TALK MONEY TO ME

ALSO BY KELLEY KEEHN

Protecting You and Your Money
A Canadian's Guide to Money-Smart Living
The Money Book for Everyone Else
She Inc.
The Prosperity Factor for Kids
The Woman's Guide to Money
The Prosperity Factor for Women

TALK
MONEY
TO ME

HOW TO SAVE, SPEND, AND FEEL GOOD ABOUT YOUR MONEY DURING COVID AND OTHER TIMES OF FINANCIAL DISTRESS

KELLEY KEEHN

Published by Simon & Schuster

New York   London   Toronto   Sydney   New Delhi

SIMON &
SCHUSTER
CANADA

Simon & Schuster Canada
A Division of Simon & Schuster, Inc.
166 King Street East, Suite 300
Toronto, Ontario M5A 1J3

Interior book design by Joy O'Meara

Manufactured in the United States of America

1 3 5 7 9 10 8 6 4 2

Library and Archives Canada Cataloguing in Publication

Title: Talk money to me: how to save, spend, and feel good about your money during Covid and other times of financial distress / Kelley Keehn.
Names: Keehn, Kelley, 1975- author.
Description: Simon & Schuster Canada edition. | Originally published: Toronto, Ontario: Simon & Schuster Canada, 2019.
Identifiers: Canadiana 20200346695 | ISBN 9781982117573 (softcover)
Subjects: LCSH: Finance, Personal—Canada.
Classification: LCC HG179 .K4285 2021 | DDC 332.02400971—dc23

ISBN 978-1-9821-1757-3
ISBN 978-1-9821-1755-9
ISBN 978-1-9821-1756-6 (ebook)

To J.R. Lakusta (Uncle John)

I told you I'd dedicate my next book to you.
I only wish you were alive to see it completed.
Thank you for helping move my familly up the pyramid.

And Kathleen Keehn

My hero, angel, and greatest teacher.

Author's Note

While all of the stories and anecdotes described herein are based on true experiences, the names, situations, and some details have been altered to protect individual privacy. Neither the author nor the publisher is engaged in rendering legal, accounting, financial, or other professional services by publishing this book. As a precaution, each individual situation should be addressed with an appropriate professional to ensure adequate evaluation and planning are applied. The author and publisher specifically disclaim any liability, loss, or risk that may be incurred as a consequence, directly or indirectly, of the use and application of any of the contents of this work. The material in this book is intended as a general source of information only and should not be construed as offering specific tax, legal, financial, or investment advice. Every effort has been made to ensure that the material is correct at the time of publication.

Interest rates, market conditions, tax rulings, and other investment factors are subject to rapid change. Individuals should consult with their personal tax advisor, Chartered Professional Accountant, Certified Financial Planner, Chartered Financial Analyst, or legal professional before taking any action based upon the information contained in this book.

Contents

TALK
MONEY
TO ME

Introduction

I've made a career out of talking about money because I want people to feel good about it, and you can't feel good about something unless you understand it. Whether you were on top of your financial life or not quite there yet, COVID-19 threw a stick of dynamite into the world's finances, not just yours. Nobody wanted to talk about money before the pandemic and for the first time, many Canadians have found themselves needing to have many uncomfortable conversations. Many had no other option but to call up their banks and ask for payment deferrals because they had lost their jobs or had depleted their rainy-day funds (if they had any). Money continues to be the leading cause of stress in our lives, but ignoring your financial situation will never make it better.

I'm here to help. Will you be brave enough to let me walk you through these chapters to reclaim ownership over your finances? I promise you, you can! With some work and the right tools, you can feel good about your money, no matter how much you have.

I'll be the first to admit it. There have been years in my life where not only was I not confident about money, I made just about every mistake you can imagine. I've learned from my missteps and from thousands of people with whom I've worked over the last number of decades. I hope by sharing my insights through the composite characters in this book, I can help you avoid the painful lessons that I, some of my past clients, and readers have endured. And I assure you; you won't find any finger-wagging or guilt trips about what you have or haven't done.

I have another confession to make. For most of my adulthood, and even now, I still struggle with what I call a "poor kid syndrome." When I was eight years old, my parents split up, and suddenly my siblings and I were being raised by a single mother on the poverty line. My mother is an incredibly generous and wise woman, but she was raising three kids on her own with zero spousal support. She had previously given up continuing her education and her career to stay at home for our family, so when my father left, my mother began working as a dishwasher and then a waitress at a pancake house a few blocks from home. That's what she could get with her limited skill set and education at the time. Money became a ruling force in our house—it was clear when we had it and abundantly obvious when we didn't. There was limited government assistance, and even when my mother did briefly accept aid, she felt stripped of her dignity and became trapped in a hellish catch-22 of either being stuck with the meagre support forever or giving it up before she could regain solid financial footing.

I saw firsthand that people make poor decisions when they don't have access to all that they need to survive and thrive in the world. COVID put a magnifying glass on everyone's financial situations. After decades of working as a personal finance educator, I see that people aren't able to do their best work or pursue their passions when they're too worried about the four-letter word that nobody wants to talk about: debt. Growing up, I remember watching my mother struggle, but I had little context or understanding. I overheard teary conversations between my mother and her girlfriends about how much she wanted off of government assistance, and yet she earned more money by not working at all than she did by working more than fifty hours a week between her waitressing and dishwashing jobs. She wanted her autonomy and freedom so desperately but felt trapped by the government aid.

While I'm keenly aware of how our system makes it difficult for people at the bottom rung to move up, I'm happy to say that it's possible to escape poverty. It's possible to find that financial freedom. I know because I escaped it, my mother escaped it, and you can too.

When I was in the financial industry, I advised many clients with varying levels of wealth over the years, and I saw that happiness and prosperity come at every point on the spectrum. In fact, several years ago I had two clients with very different definitions of prosperity, and it really made me rethink how I talk and feel about money. The first client was worth over $50 million and had no immediate family members to inherit any of it. When I met him, he was in his eighties, and he still managed his finances with the extreme frugality he learned while living through the Depression—he lived in constant fear of being on the verge of poverty, no matter how much wealth he accumulated. The second client, on the other hand, netted $1 million a year for ten years but spent lavishly. He loved entertaining, he had two Mercedes, and he had gone through two expensive divorces. By the time I met him, he was millions of dollars in debt, but you'd never guess it based on appearance alone. Both clients were using their money in ways that brought them joy, yet neither was using it to its full potential. They needed my guidance to help them find a balance between earning, saving, and spending to truly feel good about money.

After helping those clients and hundreds of others, I decided to sell my company and start educating people full-time. In the last fifteen years as a personal finance educator, the number one question I get asked is, "How is everyone else making it?" Well, I'm here to tell you that they probably aren't "making it." Before COVID, more than half of Canadians were just $200 away from being unable to pay their bills, and one in five couldn't afford to live for a week if their primary source of income disappeared. Many Canadians clearly don't feel good about money or their financial situation, and if you also feel this way, I want to let you know that it's not all your fault.

You may have heard that incentives drive the market, but right now, I'd argue that very low interest rates are driving the market, and with low interest rates come high levels of debt. To add to that, housing prices have soared because borrowing money is relatively cheap and people have easy access to lines of credit. And with a line of credit, you can make interest-only payments and have that debt stay with you forever. It's cheap money, why not indulge? And therein lies the problem: we're encouraged to spend more and use borrowed money if we have to! It's good for the economy; it's good for politicians; it's good for banks and their stockholders. Spoiler alert: it's not good for you.

I can't control how you spend your time, but I can talk about money (in the hopes of improving your understanding of financial concepts) all day, and throughout the book I'll help you understand whom you can trust with your money. I understand why you might be afraid of choosing the wrong person to meet your financial needs, so I'll show you how to create and find the right support when you need it. You'll learn how to empower yourself to interview the financial professionals you'll need along the way on your journey to financial wellness.

I strongly believe in the power of financial literacy, and I wouldn't be writing this book if I didn't think it would make a difference in someone's life, but you have to want to make a change to experience success. Given the fact that you've made it this far into the introduction, I'd say you're ready to learn, and by the end of the book, you'll be ready to put your newfound financial literacy to use. I write this not as someone who has always made the right financial decisions but as someone who has learned from past mistakes. I now have a happy relationship with money, and I'd like to help you get there too.

In this book, I do my best to dispel some of the confusion around personal finances. And, if you're like the millions of Canadians that got knocked down financially, I'm going to help you pick yourself back up. If you're struggling during COVID or from mortgage deferrals, missing credit card payments, or drowning in new debt, skip ahead to chapters 10 and 11. Once you've read those, circle back to the beginning for the basics.

No matter where you're at or why you're coming to this book, know this: The pandemic is not your fault and you're not alone if your financial situation has worsened. It's not hopeless and you can get back on track. But it may bring you comfort to know that according to a recent survey:

- 82 percent of respondents experienced a loss of income due to COVID-19
- Only 12 percent had three months' savings before the pandemic hit
- 20 percent had to take a loan to cover their expenses due to COVID-19

- 32 percent expect to add more debt to their credit cards, and
- 63 percent expect to miss paying some bills during the crisis.[1]

I know I'm not the first person to compare financial health to physical health, but hear me out, because I think it's a worthwhile comparison. Throughout the book, I'll recommend that you reach out to a professional in certain situations where advice tailored to your specific financial issues will greatly benefit you. I work with a nutritionist for this very reason because I have specific health issues and a demanding work schedule that require a tailored health regime. My nutritionist, Jocelyn, understands that results come from incremental, consistent changes that will create a healthier lifestyle—which is no different from how you'll see results in your financial life. I can get more sleep, find fifteen minutes for my daily meditation, and make an effort to regularly work out or, at the very least, walk around the block, and I'll know that I've made a difference in my health without drastically changing my routine. This is self-efficacy at its finest—these doable changes allow me to believe in my ability to achieve a goal—and I hope it's an approach that makes your financial goals seem possible.

Just as Jocelyn would never ask me to try a new fad diet that requires severe restrictions or counting calories, I'm not going to ask you to create a budget. Asking you to account for every dollar you spend for the rest of your life sounds about as sustainable as asking me to count every calorie I ingest for the rest of my life— essentially, it sounds impossible and impractical. I'm more concerned about giving you the tools necessary to create long-term change. So I promise not to tell you to make a budget. Instead, I'll ask you to put in some work, make better choices, and create awareness, but it'll never be about making sacrifices. You need to have fun with your money, so I'll teach you exercises in awareness and behavioural change that will empower you to save and spend responsibly.

You'll come to learn that I am a little odd as you read the book, so there's no sense in hiding it from you now. One (among several) of my oddities is that I have thought about the following two quotations every day of my life for the past fourteen years:

> The definition of insanity is doing the same thing over and over again and expecting a different result.
> —ATTRIBUTED TO ALBERT EINSTEIN

This first quote speaks to me because it addresses two common human tendencies: stubbornness and a hesitancy toward change based on the possibility of failure. The human brain has evolved to prefer comfort to discomfort, so it's only natural that we avoid stressful situations and challenging environments in order to stay within our comfort zones. It's tempting and easy to keep doing the same thing over and over again, and I find that people tend to avoid the possibility of failure (which nobody likes) and maintain their comfort levels (which our brains love) at all costs. But over the years, while thinking about this quote, I've realized that we also open ourselves up to criticism (which people hate) when we do something different in the hopes of seeing a new result (which is scary in itself). It's normal to crave social acceptance, so it can be unnerving to go against expectations by saving money, dressing for the job you want even if you're unemployed, asking for that raise, or buying flowers for yourself. After years of thinking about this first quote, I am here to tell you that I believe in you: embrace change as you work toward creating a better financial life for yourself.

> We cannot solve problems with the same level of
> thinking that created them.
> —ATTRIBUTED TO ALBERT EINSTEIN

This second quotation is a kind of solution to the first: we need an outside force to show us the solution to our problems. This is where I come in! I'm so excited to provide you with insight and guidance to help you think differently about money, celebrate what you're doing right, and recognize what's holding you back from change.

You might be suffering from a huge loss, a business going bankrupt, the fallout of being a victim of fraud, or maybe you're simply spending your money too quickly. With the right attitude, whatever you're going through can serve as a catalyst for building financial resiliency. As you read this book and start working on rebuilding financial stability, imagine you're earning points on your financial loyalty card—you know those customer loyalty cards you have for your favourite smoothie place or coffee shop? It's like that, but instead of spending money to get points, you're saving money! If I could be there to give you a gold star every time you learned from my advice, I would, but since I can't be there, every time you perform a task that contributes to your financial well-being, imagine checking off a box on your card.

I truly just want Canadians to be happy, especially when it comes to their financial well-being, and I don't mean that you need a lot of money to be happy. While research shows that there is indeed a correlation between happiness and income, the increase in happiness levels out around $75,000 a year. So while money might not buy you happiness, for every extra $10,000 you earn each year, your level of happiness can grow until you reach a $75,000 annual income. That being said, research has also shown that if you win the lottery, six months after winning, your level of happiness will return to your pre-jackpot baseline. The relationship between money and happiness is complex, but it is my belief that if you gather the required knowledge and skills to manage whatever income you have, you'll be able to feel good about money.

The journey won't always be easy, but you owe it to yourself to live your life with a firm financial foundation. With the right tools, you can pass on a solid financial foundation (in both wealth and wisdom) to your family and friends. I assure you that success in money matters is sustainable and can lead to a happier life. If you work to empower yourself with the necessary strategies, and open your eyes to the tricks and tactics available to you, you'll be richer in knowledge and wealth by the end of this book.

Here's to your new and continued prosperity—let's talk about money!

(1)

Cash or Credit?

Lately, I've been noticing that stores are starting to accept only credit card payments, which always makes me stop in my tracks. I remember when stores accepted only cash, but that already feels antiquated. I don't think either extreme is in anyone's best interest, but it does raise the question of how do you determine when to use cash and when to use a card. I hope you're not paying for everything in cash, but as I will advise throughout this book, it's best to find the right balance.

Ian has always been good at saving money. He had a part-time job throughout undergrad and worked full-time during the summers to save enough for tuition. He was always frugal, and as far as he knows, he did everything right with his money. His hard work meant he didn't need to take out any student loans. Some of his friends already had credit cards, but he was not tempted by aggressive credit offers from banks—instead, Ian had a second card from his mom's account that he could use in case of emergencies.

Otherwise, Ian only used cash and debit cards. He bought something only if he could afford it.

Now, Ian lives with his friends but wants to get an apartment of his own with the hope that Crystal, his girlfriend, will move in with him. Unfortunately, he just found out that a landlord will be looking for a high credit score, and he doesn't even have a credit file. Everyone keeps asking for a credit check, but he has no credit to check!

Crystal keeps hitting roadblocks on her own foray into adulthood as well. She doesn't have enough experience yet to land her dream job, so she's thinking of starting her own business as a freelancer. She needs some starting capital, but the bank has refused her a loan because she has no credit. Her cellphone is still on her parents' plan, and she, like Ian, has never had her own credit card. She'll need a car for her business, but now she's wondering if she'll even be approved for a car loan without this seemingly requisite credit.

WHERE THEY WENT WRONG

Growing up, Ian always thought that cash was king, but he is rapidly learning that is not always the case. While it still makes sense to use cash at points in your life, not having any established credit or access to a credit card will quickly limit what is available to you as you navigate toward independence. There will be several times in your life when it might not be possible to save up for what you want (or even need)—like a new house or a car, for example. There are also some things that cash simply can't buy anymore.

While Ian and Crystal are doing all the right things to avoid accumulating debt, they need to think about their future. Obtaining credit and building a great credit score will help them now and in the future. Credit cards don't have to create unnecessary debt, and the reality is that we are moving rapidly into a cashless society. Without establishing a strong credit history, it will be difficult to get approval for major purchases or rentals. Plus, there are several advantages to using plastic, especially if you pay your bills off fully and on time.

Misstep #1: Heading Out into the World without (Good) Credit

Good credit will afford you more than just being able to buy a snack on a plane throughout your life. By not having any established credit, Ian and Crystal can't gain any independence. Their credit will be checked (and required to be good) time and time again—when Ian tries to rent his own apartment, when Crystal gets her own cell phone, and when they apply for their car and home insurance, for example. A poor credit score will impede both big and small goals. Thankfully, having no credit is not as hard to correct as having a low score. If you, like Ian and Crystal, are just starting to build a life for yourself, it's important to understand the importance credit plays in Canada. You need to learn how to play the game effectively for you and your family's future.

Misstep #2: Not Getting Your Own Credit Card

Ian had access to a credit card that looks like it is uniquely his, which he mistakenly thought was helping him build credit. However, it was in fact a supplementary card for his mom's account—she can get as many supplementary cards as she'd like, which is often the case for spouses, children, or personal assistants. A supplementary credit card can be helpful if you want your child to be able to make emergency purchases. In Canada, you need to be eighteen to apply for a card, so someone who is underage can get a card only if it's attached to an adult's account, as was the case with Ian's first credit card. Or perhaps you and your spouse love reward points and you're consolidating your spending on one account to maximize the benefits and minimize account fees. This makes sense, but again, it's important to be aware that only the credit of the primary cardholder will be impacted—positively or negatively.

Although it's a supplementary card, Ian understandably thought that it was his own—supplementary cards will have your name on them, as well as a unique card number and PIN. However, Ian was not building credit in his own name. In fact, there's no record of his card activity on his credit report. If you don't apply for the card, its activity will not be reported on your credit file, which means it won't help (or hurt) your credit. Unfortunately, this also means that if the supplementary cardholder racks up a bunch of charges, there are only repercussions for the primary cardholder. It's important that you trust the person to whom you're giving a supplementary card and that they'll respect your limits. The good news is that you can cap how much your supplementary cardholder can spend. If you have a card with a $5,000 limit, for example, you can choose to get a supplementary card on your account with a limit of $1,000. You can of course also cancel the second card at any time.

If you, like Ian, are dependent on someone else's account as the supplementary cardholder, you should work toward getting your own card to build a credit file and to use in case of emergencies, especially if you're hoping to become more independent.

Misstep #3: Not Knowing When You're Building Credit

Ian and Crystal didn't know they had to build credit, let alone what contributes to a credit score, so let's try to clear that up. You'll pay a lot of bills over the course of your life, so knowing which ones contribute to building your credit is helpful. Here's a handy checklist:

Bill	Does It Affect Your Credit Report?
Mortgage	Yes*
Line of credit	Yes
Credit card(s)	Yes
Student loans	Yes
Car loans	Yes
Cell phone	Sometimes**
Gas and electric	No***
Bank account	No***
Car, house, or tenant's insurance	No
Prepaid credit card	No
Debit card	No
Supplementary credit card	No

*If you have a mortgage today, it should appear on your credit file and count toward your score. However, because mortgage payments previously weren't reported, your credit file may not reflect mortgage payments.

**At the time of the writing of this book, only Rogers and Telus report your cell phone bills to your credit file.

***If you're late making a bill payment, it can be listed in the "collections" section of your credit file. This will affect your score. If your payments are in good standing, the bills would not be listed on your file or affect your score.

Misstep #4: Relying Solely on E-transfers, Cash, and Debit Cards

By relying solely on cash and debit cards, Ian and Crystal are able to keep a close eye on their money and never have to rely on borrowed funds. What they don't realize, however, is that there are benefits to paying with a credit card that could save them from unnecessary stress.

When you pay with a credit card, you can be confident that your purchases are safe thanks to the protection of your bank's coverage. If something goes wrong with your purchase, an item doesn't arrive, or there is any fraudulent activity on your account, you won't be held responsible (so long as you adhere to the terms and conditions of your credit card agreement). Each bank and credit card company specify the period within which you have to report a fraudulent purchase—it can range from thirty to sixty days—so it's always a good idea to check your account statements regularly. The benefit of purchase protection that comes with paying by credit card may outweigh the benefit of not borrowing money and paying by e-transfer, money wire, Western Union, Bitcoin, or another untraceable method.

As cash becomes increasingly scarce, I'd recommend that you be wary of making purchases where paying with a card is not an option. It doesn't necessarily mean that you're being scammed, but it is worth thinking twice before you make that payment.

THE SOLUTION?

There are plenty of reasons why you might be interested in building a stronger credit file: you've never had a credit card and are just starting out, you're trying to repair and rebuild your own credit, or you're just realizing you haven't been building credit for years. There are steps you can follow to set a solid foundation, but there are no fast-track hacks. A slow and steady process will win this race.

For better or for worse, your credit score is fluid. Every month, as you do the right or wrong things, it will change. If your credit score is good, keep doing what you're doing. If it's not, be patient. With the right steps, you can dramatically increase your score within six months to a year.

Step #1: Get Your First Credit Card

If you already have a bank account, that's a great place to start. They'll tell you about the process to apply for a credit card—you'll have to fill out an application form, provide photo identification, and go through a credit check—and you may be pleasantly surprised that you're offered a card with little effort. If you get declined, you can find out why. Possible reasons include you have no credit or bad credit, or your income is not high enough to qualify. No matter the case, your bank should tell you why you don't qualify and the steps you can take to rectify the situation.

If you don't currently bank with anyone, then that's your first step. If you're a student, senior, entrepreneur, or new to Canada, shop around at different banks before applying for an account or credit. Many banks have incentives for certain demographics—students may get their bank fees waived, for example—so it's worth the effort to do some research to find a bank with a mandate that suits your needs.

Finally, if you've only ever been a secondary cardholder, then it's time to get your own card!

Do I Need a Secured Card?

If your credit score has taken a severe hit or you're otherwise having trouble getting approved for a credit card, you may need to get a secure credit card at your bank or with a company like Home Trust or Refresh Financial. A secure card simply requires that you deposit money with the bank as a form of security for the bank if you're unable to make payments. If you want to get a credit limit of $300, you would need to put $300 in the bank in advance. It sounds a bit like giving yourself a prepaid credit card, but as you make your payments on time, you will be establishing credit and can work toward getting a standard credit card.

If you're looking for another way to repair or build credit, Capital One offers unsecured low-limit credit cards, which have an easier approval process and are ideal for those with a poor credit score or those just starting out.

As with all credit cards, you ideally want to use the secured card often and pay it off entirely by the due date. This is especially important when you're just starting to build your credit file or if you're working toward repairing your credit. A good trick is to buy something on your card that you would normally pay for with cash. Then, when you get home, immediately make a bill payment for the exact amount of that purchase. This will help establish your reliable credit history.

Step #2: Ask the Right Questions

When you're picking a credit card, keep in mind that there are lots of options out there—pick the one that suits you best. Here are some questions that I have found helpful in the past when getting a new credit card:

- What's the annual fee on your card?
- Should you get a low-interest-rate card?
- What rewards do you get with your card, and do they exceed the annual fee?
- If you travel with your family or for work, what are the foreign transaction fees?
- If you rent cars often, is there insurance coverage included with your card?
- What other bells and whistles are you paying for, and are they worth the annual fee?

No Fees, Please!

You can and should shop around for no-fee banking. You can absolutely negotiate your bank fees, but most people never think to ask. Often, if you have three or more products with your bank, they will waive your monthly fees. Call the eight-hundred number on the back of your debit card and see what deals you can get simply by asking.

Step #3: Use Cards Regularly, Pay Them Off, Repeat

This sounds simple and straightforward, but it's important that you make your payments on time. The tricky thing is that "on time" means different things depending on your credit card. For example, if you have a Canadian Imperial Bank of Commerce (CIBC) Visa, you bank with CIBC, and your payment is due on March 10, then you can make your payment that day before your bank's cutoff time. But if you bank with Tangerine or Bank of Montreal (BMO) and are paying your Toronto–Dominion (TD) Bank Visa, you'll want to make your payment at least three business days before the due date. Simply put, make sure you're aware of how to get your payments in on time according to your bank's standards.

Always pay the minimum every month. If you're paying $100 a month as a minimum payment, that doesn't mean you can simply pay $200 this month and not make a payment next. This will negatively impact your credit score and will put you behind on the next month's payment. That being said, if you receive some bonus money, I highly recommend you make that $200 payment, but you'll still need to pay the new minimum the next month.

Step #4: Take Advantage of the Grace Period

Does a grace period mean I get free money? Not quite. A grace period is the time between making a purchase on your credit card and actually having to pay interest on it. Depending on where you bank, you'll have twenty-one to twenty-five days where you won't incur a finance charge for purchases made, so you won't owe interest. The grace period generally starts on the first day of the billing cycle and gives you time to earn the money you've borrowed so that you can repay it by the time it's due, interest free.

Step #5: Track and Earn Points

What can your points do for you? I'll demonstrate with a little math.
Let's say a credit card offers the following:

2 points for every $1 spent
10,000 points = $100 (each point is worth $0.01)
Annual fee = $150

To breakeven, you'd have to spend $625 a month on your credit card.[2]

If that sounds doable to you, then it's worth paying the annual fees. Especially when you consider how many things you can pay for with a credit card: your cable, internet, landline, cell phone, utilities, and groceries, to name a few. As long as you're confident that you'll make your payments on time, consolidating your spending on one card can be beneficial for tracking your spending and accumulating points at the same time!

To Breakeven

To find the amount of points you would need to earn in order to breakeven, divide the annual fee by the value of each point:

Annual fee / Value of each point = Breakeven points

$150/$0.01 = 15,000 points

To find out how much you need to spend each year to breakeven, divide the breakeven points amount by the number of points earned per $1 spent:

Breakeven points / Points earned per $1 spent = Annual spending required

15,000/2 = $7,500

Finally, to find out how much you would need to spend each month in order to break-even, divide your annual spending by the twelve months in a year:

Annual spending / Calendar months = Monthly spending

$7,500/12 = $625/month

Step #6: Use Cash Sometimes

Paying with cash is still important and can actually be fun. It can be useful to dedicate at least a week every few months to mindfully spending cash, but be sure to take out a reasonable amount from your bank to avoid unnecessary ATM fees.

The main benefit of paying with cash is its tangibility. When you physically take money out of your wallet or purse, your brain registers that as a loss. When you pay with plastic—regardless of whether it's a credit or debit card—you don't feel that same loss. The newer tap-and-go feature on credit and debit cards is even worse as we barely have time to register what we spent, never mind taking the time to feel a sense of loss about it.

Keep in mind that if you are paying with cash, it can be difficult to keep track of your spending. If you're fastidious about keeping receipts and accounting for your transactions, go for it. Otherwise, consider using cash to budget your spending on a weekly or monthly basis—for your coffee or lunch purchases, for example.

Do We Get Any Privacy?

Privacy is quickly becoming an important issue when it comes to our financial security as purchases are tracked. If you have a department store credit card, the company can gather valuable information about your spending habits, and privacy experts worry that one day you'll be required to share your purchase history for life, home, and car insurance policies. In October 2018, it was revealed that Statistics Canada was going to begin monitoring Canadians' financial transaction data, including bill payments, money transfers, and credit cards payments to get a more accurate view of where our money is going.[3] Shortly afterward, Statistics Canada paused their plans amid concerns about our personal information being misused and unprotected, but this is just one example among many potential privacy breaches. The question then becomes: What are the consequences of buying something that could later be used against you?

For example, since cannabis is still not legal in most jurisdictions outside of Canada, there is concern that having a record of buying it could prohibit you from traveling beyond our borders. As a result, the Canadian federal privacy commissioner recently recommended that you use cash to purchase cannabis when the option is available, and provide as little personal information as possible. The good news is that there are steps you can take to protect your security when making certain purchases, such as using a fake name, a separate post office box, and a prepaid credit card. Whether this sounds paranoid or smart to you, it's important to at least be aware of your financial privacy when making purchases that may impact you in the future.

Step #7: Less Is More

If you limit your spending to one credit card and one debit card, you can simplify your tracking and budgeting systems. The banks will do all the work for you—many banks will chart and break down your spending habits, creating an analysis for you at no cost. This only works, though, if you consolidate your spending at one bank.

Step #8: Separate Business from Pleasure

If you're self-employed, it's best to have a separate debit and credit card for your business. This isn't always possible because a new company has no credit or track record to verify, but it's certainly worth looking into. In either case, you'll need to keep good records of your expenses. One way to do this is to place all of your receipts in a basket where you can separate them out between personal and business expenses. Or, if you prefer to stay digital, take a picture of your business receipts and email them to yourself immediately. Then, when you have time, tally your spending in a handy spreadsheet—this will be crucial around tax season!

Step #9: Be Aware of Fraudulent Purchases

You will automatically receive a certain level of fraud protection with your credit card, but you should also be diligent and protect yourself. Make it a habit to read your credit card statements regularly, and look out for purchases that you don't recognize, even if it's just a few dollars. Report any suspicious activity on your credit card or bank accounts to your financial institution immediately. You can even go so far as to set up an email or text alert for every time you use your debit or credit card. That way you instantly know if someone other than yourself made a purchase, and the reminder makes it easy to keep track of your spending.

Step #10: Explore Your Options to Build an Emergency Fund

The number one rule of personal finance is to have a comfortable amount of money set aside in case of emergency, yet so few Canadians do. Currently, only one in three Canadians would be able to pay for an unexpected car or vet bill, and one in five couldn't survive a week without going into debt if they lost their primary source of income.[4] No wonder so many people are stressed about their finances. So how do you fix that?

One way to reduce money stress, if you're able, is to have a fully funded emergency account. Ideally, three to six months of your household income should be set aside in a safe, liquid account. If you're self-employed, have a highly specialized job, or work in an unstable industry, an emergency fund should cover as much as one year of your household income.

Liquid Money?

Your investments are liquid when you can sell the assets quickly and get your money back when you need it. Your principal residence, real estate, and art are all examples of investments that aren't very liquid because they take time to sell.

An emergency account should be kept in a safe, easily accessible account that you can't just dip into on a whim, but that is not so removed from your regular banking that you couldn't access it in more than a couple of days. For example, you could keep it in a safe, a money market mutual fund, or a high-yield account within a Tax-Free Savings Account (TFSA) at your bank. While you should consider having some emergency cash at your house—just enough for you and your family to survive for three to five days—your emergency fund should not be kept as cash in your house. You can of course use a credit card for an emergency, but you should not rely on it as part of your emergency account plan.

You can, however, use a line of credit as your emergency account. A line of credit is like a credit card with no card attached to it and a much better interest rate. If you're approved for one, you can use a line of credit as an emergency fund if you just don't have the money saved up yet. Even if you've set aside enough money, you might consider using a line of credit as an emergency fund and invest the money that you've saved into something with a higher rate of return. The nice thing about a secured line of credit is that it doesn't cost you anything unless you use it.

If you have a yearly salary of $50,000 and your spouse earns $42,000 a year, you have a household income of $92,000. Six months of income would be $46,000—which is a huge chunk of change. You can see why such large portions of Canadians simply don't have this saved. If you do manage to save up $46,000, that's a large amount of money to just sit in your bank account, where it will likely earn less than 2 percent interest. Over time and depending on your ability to handle risk, that money might be more wisely invested into bonds, stocks, mutual funds or exchange-traded fund (ETFs). If you're able, then it makes sense to invest those funds and rely on a line of credit if an emergency were to arise.

Step #11: Get Credit Before You Need it

It's easy to think badly about bankers, but banks and bankers aren't bad or good. They're in the business of making money. Unfortunately, when you need money, it doesn't make good business sense for bankers to give it to you. So even though it seems a bit backward, you can apply for extra money before you actually need it.

If you have a solid job and are in a good financial position, I'd suggest that you apply for a line of credit while you're still attractive to a bank. As soon as you're unemployed, no matter your current endeavour, the bank will not think of you as a profitable investment. Many people are under the false impression that their past years of steady employment will help them even after they've left their job, but your bank won't take that into account. Hopefully, you will never need the line of credit, but at least it's there if you ever want it. Whether it's to start your own business, take maternity or paternity leave, go on a sabbatical, or go back to school, a line of credit will wait until your time of need.

Step #12: Know Yourself

The most important advice in this entire chapter is to know your own limits. If having easy access to credit will be too much of a temptation, then you should respect that because only 56 percent of Canadians pay their credit cards off fully each month and have zero interest costs.[5] If you fall within the 44 percent of Canadians who don't pay off a credit card every month, you can make adjustments to suit your needs. A low- or no-annual-fee card with a low interest rate may be best for you, and you might also consider setting a low credit limit on your card or getting a consolidation loan. The good news is that you can also use other means to build your credit beyond a traditional credit card, including government student loans, lines of credit, and car loans.

Credit Report 101

What Is a Credit Report?

Your credit report is a snapshot of your relationship with your past and current debts, and it exists whether you're aware of it or not. In early 2018, a major Equifax breach in Canada and the US caused quite a shock for many people, as it was the first they'd heard that their sensitive information is housed at two reporting agencies: Equifax and TransUnion in Canada (there are three in the US). However, the fine print on the paperwork for your credit card, loan, or mortgage indicates that you're agreeing that your lender can do a credit check. You also agree that your lender can peek into your credit file periodically to see if they should increase or decrease your original credit limit. Your lender can even take your credit away entirely if your credit score drops dramatically.

Demand Loan?

A demand loan is a debt where the creditor can request that you pay your balance in full immediately at any time. If you've been behind on payments for your credit card or line of credit, for example, your lender may take action. They can also get a sense of how well you're paying your other debts by checking your credit report. If they see a pattern of late payments, they're well within their rights (which are detailed in your terms and agreements) to demand payment in full. These situations are rare but do happen!

What's on Your Report?

Reading your credit report might seem intimidating at first, but it's simpler than it looks. Here are the main takeaways:

- **Personal information.**
  - Your name
  - Partially blocked social insurance number (SIN)
  - Partially blocked out date of birth
  - Current and previous addresses
  - Current employment information
- **Debt information.** A list of debts, including those you're still paying off. Every six or seven years, your old debts no longer factor into your score, but they may still appear on your report. This section will include:
  - The amount you borrowed
  - The balance on the account
  - The number of times you were thirty, sixty, or ninety days late (if any)
  - Other details pertaining to that debt
- **Collections accounts.** If you've ever defaulted on your debts and had something fall into collections, it would show here. If you have something "in collections," a debt is outstanding and grossly overdue—it usually takes ninety days or more for your lender to write off a debt and send it to a collection agency to try to recoup the funds.
- **Credit inquiries to the file.** Here, you'll see who's been looking at your report, broken out into two types of inquiries:
  - Hard inquiries, which can count against your score, result from actively seeking credit. If you apply for a new car loan, credit card, or even cell phone, you agree to have a credit check

performed, and it would appear on your credit score as a hard inquiry.

- Soft inquiries do not count against your score but will still appear on your report. These result from you or a company checking your credit as part of a background check. This could be your credit card company checking in to see if they want to offer you a credit increase or a result of checking your own credit report. You can check your credit report as often as you like without it affecting your score.

Within the last few years your mortgage and some cell phone accounts as well as your home phone have been added to credit reports and may now factor into your score. However, not all lenders have updated their systems to reflect these changes, so don't be alarmed if you don't see these on your report.

What's Not on Your Credit Report?

If you're concerned about companies having access to your information, you can rest assured that none of the following are listed on your report: income, net worth, or a list of your assets. Your credit report is only a reflection of your credit history, not an entire picture of your financial life.

What Does Your Score Mean?

Credit scores range from 300 to 900. While high scores are the most favourable, only an estimated 5 percent of Canadians have a score over 850, and it's the range that matters not the actual number. If your score is 791, you are no worse off than someone's score of 859 because you would both fall within the 790–860 range. Your report will indicate where your score stands in the following ranges: Poor, Fair, Good, Very Good, or Excellent. The higher your score, the more likely you are to be approved for that loan, rental, or new cell phone. Keep in mind that if you order a free report via the mail or a basic report online, your score will not be listed, so it won't be as useful. I'd suggest always paying for the full report.

Can You Still Get Declined with a Good Score?

Lenders look at more than just your credit score, so they can absolutely decline your request even if you have a good score. If you have a low income or too much debt, or you are self-employed, a high score might not be enough. Or if you're shopping for too much credit in a short period of time—if you move to a new city and apply for a new car, line of credit, and laptop lease within a few weeks—you may also be declined. The credit reporting agency's system may think you're in financial trouble once they see that you are applying for so many things in such a short period of time. Ideally, you should try to space out your applications for credit.

What Can You Do to Improve Your Score?

There are steps you can take to raise your score, but it's important to know that there is no guaranteed fix. Both Equifax and TransUnion have proprietary algorithms that factor in varying aspects of your financial history to determine your score. If you follow these suggestions, though, you should be able to improve your score within six months to a year.

- Make your bill payments on time, every time.
  - If you're only paying your minimum payment, paying it regularly and on time is more important and effective than paying more

money in one month but missing the minimum payment the next month.

- Avoid having anything in collections. If you do (maybe you forgot to make a final payment on your cable bill before you moved), you'll have to work with the creditor to come to an agreement and work with Equifax and/or TransUnion to have it removed.
- If you have a dispute with a creditor (your car lease company or your cell phone provider, for example), continue to make your minimum monthly payments on time. Once you've resolved your dispute, you can try to get your money back, but stopping payments will affect your score and show up as a late payment on your report, which can be nearly impossible to have removed.
- Keep your credit account balance as low as possible—ideally, within 50 percent of your available limit. If you have a credit card with a $5,000 limit, try to keep your balance below $2,500. If you're always maxed out on your credit, that will hurt your score over time.
- Don't close out a credit card account that you've had for a long time, even if you're no longer using it. An account with a long history helps your score. Use the card periodically and pay it off in full. If the cost of the annual fee is an issue, talk to your bank about having it switched to a no-fee card without changing the account.
- Initially, a new loan or fully funded line of credit (for example, if you were using a line of credit to pay for a kitchen renovation) can bring down your score because it will be seen as credit that is at full capacity on your report. Make regular, timely payments, and your score will gradually increase.
- Sometimes having too much available credit, even if all your balances are low or at zero, can lower your score. Theoreti-

cally, you could use up all that credit tomorrow, so try to avoid having multiple credit cards or loans.

- Don't apply for department store credit cards—the ones that offer you 15 percent or 20 percent off your purchase when you're about to pay if you apply for their card. These hurt your score because the credit agencies' algorithm is skeptical of any credit cards with a 29 percent annual interest rate when you could get a card with a much better interest rate at your bank. The credit reporting agencies may assume that you were denied credit cards with a better rate, and your score reflects that.
- Don't avoid credit. You need it to build a score and credit history.
- Don't rely on a supplementary card as your only credit card. They will not help you build credit.

Keep in mind that one wrong or right move is not going to change your score dramatically in the short-term. It's all about consistency and making payments on time.

If you feel like your credit rating is unsalvageable, you may want to seek out a nonprofit credit counsellor. Be cautious of shady businesses trying to sell a quick fix to your debt and credit problems because it won't be that simple. If you choose a nonprofit credit counsellor, they will review your credit report and score with you at no cost, and will guide you on the best path to rectifying your financial situation.

WHERE ARE THEY NOW?

Ian and Crystal both applied for credit cards and were approved quickly by their banks. Ian stopped using his mother's supplementary card, and both he and Crystal have been using the cards in their own names, building up their credit for over two years now.

With the help of his mother's agreeing to cosign, Ian got an apartment of his own, and Crystal worked part-time jobs until she was able to get approved for a loan to start her own business. After years of being so diligent with using only cash or debit cards, they are both pleasantly surprised by the switch to credit. By making most of their purchases on a credit card, Ian and Crystal are able to review spending at the end of the month easily in two consolidated statements. They've even taken a trip to see Crystal's parents on Prince Edward Island by using the points they've earned from their cards—a goal they didn't think they'd achieve for another three years.

They are working toward bigger goals now that they have established strong credit scores, like buying a car and saving up for a house. Their hard work is paying off—Crystal's bank has even suggested she can get a line of credit to expand her business. Once a month, Ian and Crystal still enjoy using cash, making a game of it to keep track of their spending habits and remind themselves of the tangibility of money.

2

Shopaholic Anonymous

Spending your hard-earned money is easier than ever, with online shopping, phone apps, every kind of food ordering service, and the ability to pay for things in store with just a tap of your cell phone. With all of these services, it's easy to lose track of how much you're spending, and it's tempting to just say yes—to that new outfit, the fancy latte, or the condo you can't afford.

As much as Jessica hates to admit it, she feels like the quintessential millennial as she succumbs to the temptations around her, no matter the cost. She's been splurging to her heart's desire for years, she is swimming in student loan and credit card debt, and shopping is her favorite hobby. She works as an assistant marketing manager at a Toronto start-up, where she earns barely enough to pay the bills every month. Each year, she seems to creep deeper into debt. And retail therapy isn't helping.

Now, she is in real trouble. This is the third time in seven years that she is being pushed out of her Toronto condo. The cost of rent is only increasing, and her landlords are getting greedy—wanting to remodel in order to charge considerably more rent. She hasn't added up the numbers yet, but she knows that the cost of moving can be detrimental and will practically drain her meager emergency savings. She's already paying for basics, including groceries, with her credit card. She always finds a way to make her payments, but never more than the minimum, and she's often a few days late.

As she is once again kicked out of her place, Jessica feels like she's living in the episode of *Sex and the City* where Carrie is almost forced out of her Manhattan apartment because she can't afford to buy it, and yet she has over $40,000 worth of shoes in her closet. Watching that scene play out on screen was entertaining, but living the real thing is an entirely different feeling, especially now that she's packing up her belongings—countless shoes included.

WHERE SHE WENT WRONG

Jessica is not alone in this feeling of drowning in consumer- and student-loan debt. Right now, about a third of Canadians have over $22,000 in debt beyond their mortgages.[6] It quickly becomes very expensive to be broke, and if you're only paying the minimum payments, you're only paying down the interest and not the principal. With a little bit of work, and the willingness to get better, Jessica—and you—can come out on top.

Misstep #1: Paying Only What's Requested

What is the impact of making only the minimum payment on your credit card? The average person in our country has a balance of approximately $4,000 on their credit card, while only 56 percent of Canadians claim to pay their balances off every month.[7]

If you have a balance of $4,000 on a high-interest-rate credit card—let's suppose your interest rate is 29 percent—how long do you think it would take you to pay it off? How much interest would it cost you? Let's calculate that together, assuming you don't make any new purchases while paying it off:

Only making the minimum payment (approximately $120) each month?

Time to pay off card	41 years and 2 months
Original balance	$4,000.00
Interest paid	$15,542.93
Total paid	$19,542.93
Amount saved	-
Time saved	-

A credit card balance of $4,000 at a 29 percent interest rate would have a minimum monthly payment of $120, which will decrease as your balance decreases. If you pay only your monthly minimum, it will take a shocking forty-one years to pay off the card, and you'll have spent $15,542.93 for that original $4,000.00.

Making the minimum payment plus an additional $5 each month?

Time to pay off card	22 years and 9 months
Original balance	$4,000.00
Interest paid	$10,362.41
Total paid	$14,362.41
Amount saved	$5,180.52
Time saved	18 years and 5 months

With only $5 more a month—yes, just $5 a month—you can cut the time it will take you to pay off $4,000 in half! That being said, over twenty-two years is still a long time to be making payments!

Paying a fixed amount ($200) each month?

Time to pay off card	2 years and 4 months
Original balance	$4,000.00
Interest paid	$1,531.34
Total paid	$5,531.34
Amount saved	$14,011.59
Time saved	38 years and 10 months

By bumping up your payment to $200 a month, you'll be rid of this pesky debt in just two years and four months. Sounds like magic, right? And, you'll save a whopping $14,000 and change by doing so. That's only $80 more a month than the minimum payment and less than $3 extra a day. See what a little number crunching can do to motivate you to pay your debt sooner?

By paying only the minimum payment on your credit cards, your bank and credit card company profit while you continue to lose money. It's so important that you understand this, that in 2009 the Canadian government legislated that credit card companies provide calculations on your statement each month showing how long it would take to repay the total balance if only the minimum payment is made every month. And yet, very few people really read through their monthly bills—especially when their bills outweigh their income each month.

Misstep #2: Forgetting about Dormant or Rarely Used Credit Cards

Jessica had completely forgotten about her department store credit card until she received an "urgent" letter in her inbox one day alerting her that she was late to pay the annual membership fee. The letter contained aggressive wording and warned of increasing collections and legal action. The annual membership fee was only $140!

Unfortunately, it doesn't matter if the amount due was $14 or $14,000—no matter the cost, if you're late paying a bill, you'll likely find yourself in a financial bind. Usually, collections requests become aggressive ninety days after a missed payment. Make sure to check both your physical mailbox as well as your email inbox every month. If you're missing a bill, don't assume that you've been sent a gift by the bank gods. It could be a sign of fraudulent activity. Fraudsters may divert mail from you in order to apply for credit in your name only to then have the mail forwarded to their address. More important, keeping track of your bills is a good way to stay on top of recurring payments and due dates.

It's also a good idea to inspect the details of all your bank and credit card accounts. This will ensure that unexpected fees or rate increases don't creep up on you. If you miss one or two payments on your credit card, the bank can increase your 18 percent interest rate to a 28 percent interest rate until your next six months of payments are made on time. As another example, if you consistently max out your cards, you can be dinged with an over-limit fee, which is $29 at minimum. All of these costs add up quickly after just a few months of not making payments on time or being over limit.

Paperless?

Should you go paperless? Opting for paperless bills is both great for the environment and can protect you from fraudsters infiltrating your physical mail. However, as you work toward overseeing your budget, remember that going paperless means you'll have to go online and check your accounts regularly. If you do choose to go paperless, consider adding a monthly reminder in your calendar to check your online statements—from your bank, but also other recurring bills such as your cell phone, internet, and hydro—if you're not receiving email notifications from the companies directly.

Money Stress?

If you're stressed about money, you're not alone: 41 percent of Canadians rank money as their main cause of stress, more so than concerns about health, relationships, or their jobs.[8] But under too much stress, you can suffer from what's called a *bandwidth tax*. You know when you have countless programs running at the same time and your computer just can't handle one more request, so it finally shuts everything down? That happens with your brain too. Your cognitive capacity to address the many demands in your life does not always leave room for thinking about things such as saving for an emergency fund or for your future. You might be dedicating so much time to planning your kid's upcoming field trip that your brain is so filled with worry you have no time or headspace to think about saving money.

If you're stressed about money, the first step is to acknowledge the issue and be kind to yourself as you work through your financial problems. Find or create a support group—whether it's in real life or online. Reach out to a professional—a banker, a Certified Financial Planner, an accountant, or a nonprofit credit counsellor. Ideally, do all of this before the situation is dire.

Above all else, remember that self-worth and net worth are very distinct things. You're still a whole and valuable person, regardless of your money situation. When you remind yourself of that, it can be a little easier to act.

Misstep #3: Eating the Whole Pie

You've done it, I've done it, and Jessica does it a lot. You know how you feel when you're on a diet, wanting to fit into that outfit for a special occasion, but you finally cave to the temptations around you? You made a goal and set good intentions, but you've had a bad day—your boss yelled at you and your dog threw up in your shoes—and suddenly you can't see what's so bad about eating the whole tub of ice cream your spouse bought last week.

Once you give in to temptation, your sugar craving likely returns with a vengeance the next day. Now you don't just feel bad about what happened yesterday, but you've set yourself up to repeat the habit today, and likely tomorrow. You have a new baseline for what's permissible. If you're used to eating only one piece of pie but then you eat the entire pie in one sitting, you can later justify that eating only two pieces is demonstrating self-control. This justification of overindulgence happens with spending too. If you've ever been on a shopping binge, you'll recognize this behaviour.

If you splurge too often on nonnecessities, you start to rationalize overspending as normal; the same way we can rationalize overeating. The obvious advice here is to keep track of your spending, and if you are a victim of creeping financial obesity, take a time-out. Absence really does make the heart grow fonder—or at least more appreciative in times of overspending. Aim to go a few days a week without buying any "wants" to avoid overindulging.

Misstep #4: Lured by Sales

If you're a bargain shopper, you're not going to like this tip. I'm sorry to be the one to tell you that sales and discounts provide a lot of revenue for retailers, and are a means to entice you to buy things you don't need. Don't get me wrong: if you're buying an expensive item like a new TV, mattress, or a car, keeping an eye out for great sales is certainly worthwhile. But when you're walking past your favourite store and are lured in by 50-percent-off posters advertising a sale, you're probably going to spend money unnecessarily. The same goes for email alerts from your favourite stores—they know they're going to tempt you to shop with promises of deep discounts and online promotions. But do you need it? Probably not.

You are better off avoiding the temptation of sales and only buying what you really need and love, even if it's at full price. If it's going to sit in your closet or go untouched in your fridge, then it's really not a deal at all. If you love a good bargain and are still itching to shop the sales rack, you can put all that energy into saving on things that you'll always need, like staples that don't expire, and you will eventually use. Finally, be cognizant of your time: If you're going to run all over town to save a few dollars, how much of your time are you losing in pursuit of that small savings?

Misstep #5: The Deal and the Department Store Card

You've been there. You're at your favourite department store, and just as you're getting ready to pay, the salesclerk tells you about how you can get 15 percent off your entire purchase if you sign up for their store credit card. Think of the instant savings! It's what any frugal shopper would do, right? Wrong. These loyalty credit cards are bad news for your wallet and your credit score. Most have a 29 percent interest rate, so as soon as you run a balance on the card, that fifteen percent discount doesn't look so attractive. It is to the department store's benefit for you to not pay it off by the due date.

You may think that you've discovered a clever workaround to these offers: take the initial discount by signing up for the card, and then simply don't activate it when it comes in the mail a few weeks later. Unfortunately, that's not how it works. Once you apply for the card in store, you've agreed to the terms and conditions, and regardless of whether or not you activate the card, you not only have created the account, but you've also directly affected your credit score.

Misstep #6: Not Knowing What You Already Own

Do you know what's in your closet right now? What about your garage? How many little black dresses do you need? What about the shoes, fishing gear, and golf clubs that are piling up in storage? Without keeping track, we often end up unnecessarily buying duplicates of items we already own. If this sounds like you, then I'd suggest creating an inventory of your stuff—this can be as intricate as taking photos of all your clothes to create a visual reminder of your closet's contents or as simple as creating a list of items you already own. Then, the trick is to only buy items that will complement what you have. This isn't just about spending too much money on clothes. Maybe you have multiple motor-cycle helmets or three copies of the same comic book but don't know it.

Misstep #7: Retail Therapy

A good shopping spree can bring greater relief than a visit to a therapist, and retail therapy is cheaper than actual therapy, right? But if you're making those purchases with a credit card, that enjoyment will be short-lived, even if the relief is instant.

Be conscious of your spending habits and reassess why you feel that need to shop. Are you looking for some alone time—away from the house or the office? Can you find some alternative ways to satisfy the desire to reward yourself without spending? Make a list of ten to twenty low-to-no-cost ideas that you can try out before you buy out. Here are a few of my favourite alternatives:

- Go to a movie
- Peruse some magazines at your local bookstore
- Invite a friend over for a cup of tea
- Visit an art gallery
- Host a clothing swap

THE SOLUTION?

If you've ever faced stretches of overspending, it's not all your fault—it's partially your brain's doing. We are hardwired to want instant gratification, and the dopamine hit we get when we buy something can be irresistible. But you can override these impulses with rational thoughts and strategies to reduce temptation.

Step #1: Reduce or Eliminate Temptation

Disable the convenience of autopay and expediency tools offered by online retailers. You have likely shopped on websites such as Amazon that have encouraged you (and made it alarmingly easy) to have your credit card saved in their system for future purchases. The retailer is counting on the ease of "one click" shopping—helping you spend money on a whim helps them make a faster profit. If you had to step away from your computer to get your credit card out of your wallet, you might just change your mind about making the purchase. I'm not suggesting you have to get as extreme as freezing your credit cards in ice (as some experts recommend), but start by making it a little more difficult to make that impulse purchase. Put a little distance between you and your online purchases.

Step #2: Spread Out Your Purchases and Gift Giving

Sometimes shopping is inevitable, and unless you're strong enough to do a #nospendchallenge, you're bound to face bouts of necessary spending. Maybe you're going to redecorate your apartment, or your partner's love language is receiving gifts. My advice is to stagger your purchases—you'll find that doing so can bring you so much more joy. If you are redecorating, you might be tempted to buy a bunch of items at once—a new sofa, throw pillows, that industrial-looking lamp you've been eyeing—but research reveals you'll likely only enjoy those purchases for a few weeks or months, maximum. However, if you spaced out those purchases, you can experience the joy from each item, thereby maximizing your spending pleasure. Try it out the next time you're tempted to buy several things at once. And if you're lavishing your partner with gifts, each item will command more attention and appreciation when given over time.

Step #3: Intentionally Window-Shop

Are you eyeing that new pair of shoes or those Bluetooth speakers? Try enriching your experience and overall satisfaction by lengthening the buying process. You'll once again have to use a little willpower to override your default impulse for immediate gratification. If you can find a way to enjoy your shopping experience without buying the product immediately, you'll increase your pleasure. Try going out to the store without your wallet or shop online with a promise to yourself to only look. Savouring the process can often feel as good as buying if you deliberately make an activity out of it and are clear about your intentions from the start. When you shop impulsively, you rob yourself of a more intentional and thoughtful experience.

Step #4: Save Up for Impulse Buys

If you know that shopping brings you joy, then set yourself up for success. Prepare for the urge to shop by creating a separate account (or if you're feeling old-school, set aside funds in a plain old piggy bank) that you can draw from guiltlessly. If you bank online, it's relatively easy to set up a new no-fee account. Think of how fun it would be to throw caution to the wind and spend freely, knowing that you had saved up to do so! Rename your shopping savings account so every time you log in to your online banking, you can see that goal and the growing balance. This will provide you with a consistent reminder of the goal you're working toward and help delay that itch to shop until you reach a set goal.

Step #5: Create a Cooling-Off Period

Another way to curb unnecessary spending is to establish rules for yourself when shopping for things you want (rather than need). For example, set a price limit for how much you're willing to spend when you head out on a shopping trip. Then, to be sure you really want the item, wait twenty-four hours before making the purchase. Simply walking out of a store or stepping away from your computer will help you decide if you really want it. If you're still thinking about the item later when you can think more rationally, then you can make the well-considered purchase with a satisfied conscience and a happy wallet.

Step #6: Refunds Only

Get to know the return policies of the stores you frequent most often. Establish another rule that you'll only buy from stores that offer a 100 percent refund option. If you know you are going to be tempted to impulse shop, avoid shopping at stores that only offer an in-store credit. That way, if you do go on a shopping binge, when the spending hangover hits, you can return some or all of your purchases.

Step #7: Invest in Yourself

Open up an investment account, Registered Retirement Savings Plan (RRSP), or a Tax-Free Savings Account (TFSA). Even if you don't have a single dollar to invest right now, simply by opening your account, you'll create a goal and be more conscious of the need to save. Think about your financial goals the same way you might think about health goals—they're equally important to the well-being of your future self. If you set a goal to get into better shape, you might sign up for a gym membership. If you didn't use the membership, every time you passed by the gym without going in, you'd likely feel a pang of guilt. It's easy to want to avoid that guilt, so we often don't set the goal or take the first steps to achieving it. But that's just your conscience keeping your goals in check— a reminder and motivation to do something for your future self.

If you don't take that first step (whether it's opening an investment account or getting a gym membership) toward a goal, you can be blissfully ignorant about the opportunities to better yourself. However, if you'd like to make a change in your life, you need to hold yourself accountable. By opening an account, you'll commit to finding money to spend on your future self. Opening an investment account can take less than ten minutes if you already bank online, and even if you do have to go in person to set it up, that hour or two of your life is simply another investment in your future.

Once you have an account set up, add a recurring reminder in your calendar to prompt you to commit to funding your new investment account. It can be as little as $25 a month, but as your financial stability grows, so too can your monthly contribution. Eventually, you won't even notice it coming out of your account. At the end of the year, you'll be amazed by how much has accumulated.

Step #8: Figure Out Your Baseline

Your spending baseline is what you spend on all your essentials like living expenses, including transportation and family sustenance. This can be difficult to track, so you might have to do a little digging. If you save all your receipts and go through them regularly, you will be able to tally up your spending fairly easily. If you've never done this and you're not going to be convinced otherwise, you can start by putting all your spending for a year on one credit or debit card—this way your bank will do the tracking for you. As mentioned, some banks will also track all your spending and break down your purchase habits. It can be helpful to see where your money is going. The important thing is to get an understanding of how much you're spending on things you desire but don't need. If you are feeling guilty about what you see, be up-front and honest with yourself about it, but more importantly, this exercise is about setting yourself up for success with rules that you can stick to.

There are also budgeting apps that can track your spending habits if your bank doesn't offer the service, but a word of warning: if you choose to use one of these apps, you'll nullify the fraud protection you get from your bank and credit card companies. The apps will track your spending and your net-worth in real time, and all your credit cards, debit cards, and investment accounts can be linked in the app. These apps are flashy and take a lot of the effort out of money management, but I'd avoid them if you can.

Check with your own bank to see what tracking solutions they provide, and keep this in mind if you're ever shopping around to transfer to another bank. If your bank is offering a tracking solution, consider the task of monitoring your baseline made that much simpler!

WHERE IS SHE NOW?

Jessica went online and found a couple of debt-repayment calculators to open her eyes to the magic of compound interest. She set up automatic payments on all her credit cards and loan payments, and she is contributing at least an extra $50 a month to all her debts. In order to be able to afford these payments, she's instituted a cooling-out period for a few months until she feels financially stable enough to begin shopping smartly.

After assessing her baseline, Jessica realized that she was spending approximately $425 a month on unnecessary desires—half of which was going on credit cards that weren't getting paid down. She's been increasingly marketing her freelance writing and editorial services on social media, and as a result, she's bringing in an extra $300 a month in income. She has also cut her impulse purchases by $200 a month. With this extra $500 a month, Jessica is hoping to burn her debts rapidly and save up for a dream trip. If Jessica focuses on paying her high-interest-rate credit cards first, she'll be debt free years sooner and save thousands in interest. With this goal in mind, she's decided to split the $500 evenly across her two cards.

By getting mindful about her spending, Jessica realized that she's never been able to afford to travel because she's spent all her extra dollars on clothes and dining out. With the goal of going on a big adventure in the next year or two, she's set up a new bank account and named it "Jessica's Dream Vacay." She also downloaded some mindfulness apps, which she dedicates five minutes a day to using. This helps her keep herself motivated to save for her goals and grants her some of that alone time she found while shopping—but at no cost at all!

Now that's a future Jessica can get excited about—and she's one step closer to being debt free! With this new direction and commitment to financial stability, Jessica is already far from a life of six-digit debt and zero savings. There's hope that she won't be scared out of the big city after all, and she might not have to pull the moving boxes out of storage for a long while.

Leaving Money on the Table

They say that if you love what you do, you never have to work a day in your life, but we can't all be so lucky. How do you ensure that you're getting the most out of your job, even if you work to live, not live to work? It's important to understand your employee benefits (if you have them) and learn how you can expand your financial portfolio with the tools that your company makes available to you.

Lyndsay was in her office lunchroom when she first learned that she wasn't taking advantage of her company's benefits and investment opportunities. She overheard her coworkers complaining about the company's share price dipping. One coworker was worried about being able to retire with the lower share price, while another chimed in that she was using the drop in price as a buying opportunity. Over coffee that afternoon, another coworker confessed to Lyndsay that she was thinking about asking for a raise, especially since she had been putting in weekend shifts for months without getting any extra compensation.

That night, Lyndsay bombarded her partner, Terrance, with

questions, including: "Do you have a pension at work? Do you have a matching program? Why haven't we talked about this?" They had been living together for nearly five years, but neither had thought much about how they could use their work benefits to improve their finances. They are legally common-law spouses, and although Terrance knows he'll propose to Lyndsay one day, he's never felt any pressure to discuss their financial future. He's previously been married, and he has a sixteen-year-old daughter who lives with her mom. Since the divorce, he's become quite private about his finances.

Neither Lyndsay nor Terrance intended for their current job to become their career, but Lyndsay has been at the same nursing home for eleven years and Terrance has been at his advertising firm for nine years. They haven't stopped to think about planning for retirement, but maybe now's the time.

After a long post-dinner conversation about their future—as a family unit and as financially stable adults—Lyndsay and Terrance are feeling a little lost. They moved in together years ago but never really talked about what that meant. If they don't start to pay attention to their benefits and financial plans at work, they won't be prepared for retirement—together or alone. These are hard conversations that need to start with clarity as they prepare for the future.

WHERE THEY WENT WRONG

Lyndsay was lucky to overhear those conversations at work because we often don't look at our finances clearly until something forces us to do so—whether that's the loss of a job, retirement, or a disability. Lyndsay and Terrance are leaving money on the table, and you might be too!

Misstep #1: Missing Out on Free Money

When Lyndsay first qualified for her employee benefits program, she didn't take it very seriously because she didn't think she'd be at that company for very long. It's been eleven years, and she's never taken the time to revisit the plan.

If you have an employee benefits plan, don't fall into the trap of ignoring it or not getting the most out of your employer's matching program. Currently, there's an estimated three to four billion dollars unclaimed each year by employees who are not fully participating in their plans.[9] You could be missing as much as $2,000 (or more) in free money every year if you have an employee benefits program that you're not taking full advantage of.

Misstep #2: Not Understanding Their Plans

Lyndsay and Terrance never took the time to unpack the options available to them with their companies' investment plans. Do they have a defined benefit plan? A defined contribution plan? How does this affect their retirement planning? Should they be planning their future as a couple or individually? These are the questions they should have been asking years ago.

The following chart breaks down the types of benefit plans you should know about, but you should also talk to your own human resources department to find out what you're entitled to. Keep in mind, this chapter is only going to cover the financial benefits offered by employee plans, but there are often other valuable perks such as reimbursements from a health fund, as well as life and disability insurance.

Plan Type	Benefits?	When You Get the Money
Defined Benefit Plan: A pension plan in which your company guarantees your retirement payment lump-sum amount in advance. These plans are almost as rare today as a unicorn.	You and your employer invest a certain amount of money and your company provides you with a "defined benefit": a set amount of money you'll have at retirement. In the past, it was easier for pension plans to project how much an employee would require at retirement. However, because interest rates have been so low in recent decades, it's been tricky for companies to keep up with what they've promised to employees and often fall short, resulting in an "unfunded liability." Most companies have moved away from these types of plans.	You can't take money out of this plan until retirement. If you leave your employer, there are options to move the money, but there are many rules that you must adhere to according to pension legislation. If you leave before a designated time, you may not get all the benefits that your employer put in on your behalf.
Defined Contribution Plan: A pension plan in which you know what you and your employer are contributing, but there is no set amount you'll have at retirement.	These plans take a great degree of risk away for the employer because the final sum is based on investment earnings. These are still very beneficial for the employee, but require effective financial planning to ensure you are making the right investments while simultaneously saving on the side in case your plan doesn't return what you had hoped.	These plans must also adhere to pension legislation, and the ability to withdraw money from it is limited. A pension is supposed to provide income for your life at retirement, so you can't just make lump-sum withdrawals like you can with other investments. These rules are in place to protect your future self.

Plan Type	Benefits?	When You Get the Money
Group Registered Retirement Savings Plan (RRSP): A savings plan in which you contribute payments from each pay cheque, and is administered by your employer. These are the most popular with employers today.	These plans are growing in popularity because they're much easier and less expensive for an employer to set up, especially for smaller businesses that might not have the resources to set up a large-scale pension. Group RRSPs are offered on their own or in addition to another type of pension. Often, the employer will provide a matching program with RRSPs, so for every dollar you contribute, the employer will match the contribution up to a certain amount. These plans also offer a minimal management fee—the hidden fee for managing the investments within the plan—when compared to buying the same investment from a bank or other financial institution on your own. Theoretically, this provides a higher rate of return.	Group RRSPs are much more flexible, and allow you to take funds out or transfer the plan to your own financial intuition. However, some employers restrict how and when you move funds while you're employed. If you leave your company, you have to move the plan to a financial institution because the employer no longer has the responsibility to hold it.
Stock Option Plans: A benefit plan in which you can buy your company's stocks at a set or preferred price.	Although these plans are less common, they still exist, and can be a good opportunity to compensate employees.	Stock option plans can vary drastically company by company based on a number of factors, including stock price and industry—is it volatile or going through a down time, for example? Ideally, stocks are held for the long term. Your company plan will dictate how easily you can sell them, or if you need to hold on to them for a set period.

Misstep #3: Setting It and Forgetting It

Lyndsay has been contributing to her RRSP every paycheque, but she has no sense of where her money is invested. Her first mistake is that an RRSP is not an investment; it's a tax shelter. Her second mistake is that although she drops money into her plan every month, she never checks to see how it's doing. Ideally, Lyndsay should be checking on where the money is being invested and whether or not she needs to be moving it around. She set it and forgot it, but that works best with a slow cooker, not your money!

Misstep #4: Using an RRSP as an Emergency Account

When Terrance had trouble coming up with money to pay his child support payments to his ex-wife, he didn't have an emergency account to rely on, so he dipped into his employer RRSP account for the funds. Unfortunately, for every time he made a withdrawal from his investments, he was hit with a withholding tax and a nasty surprise during tax season when he found out that he had to pay a heavy tax penalty for taking those funds out. He also learned the hard way that he wasn't able to put the money back into his RRSP.

Misstep #5: Not Investing in Themselves

Both Lyndsay and Terrance failed to see their careers as a million-dollar investment. Even if they earn an average salary, they will earn millions in their lifetime. Too few people recognize that a job can be an opportunity for great wealth over the span of a life. When you have a continuous stream of income, you should factor that in when making investment decisions, especially when you are given investment opportunities as an employee. Your earned income should be seen as an asset class, and never taken for granted. (More on this shortly.)

Misstep #6: No Negotiation

When Lyndsay started her job, she was young and naïve and didn't know that she could or should negotiate her salary. This mistake of not negotiating her starting salary could cost Lyndsay an estimated $500,000 by the time she is sixty years old.[10] Although men will also fail to negotiate their salary either at the beginning or throughout their career, several studies reveal that men are four times more likely to negotiate a salary than a woman.[11]

Misstep #7: Forgetting about Your Beneficiaries

After his divorce, Terrance removed his ex-wife as the beneficiary in his will and added his daughter and mother in her place. However, he forgot that his ex-wife was still listed as the beneficiary on his life insurance policy, his work pension plan, and group RRSP. If he doesn't amend those plans before he dies, his ex-wife will still receive his assets.

At the time of listing a beneficiary—the person that you name to inherit your money or other benefits when you pass away—your death might be the furthest thing from your mind, but it's important to think about. You can name a beneficiary in your will, as well as in your pension plan, RRSP, group RRSP, life insurance policies, and more. Not all assets have the ability to name a beneficiary, and when you die, these assets form your estate, which is divided among the beneficiaries listed in your will. A lack of consistency between the beneficiaries listed among your various plans and your will can create a great deal of confusion, so take the time to think about your assets. Do you know who will receive what if something were to happen to you?

THE SOLUTION?

As previously mentioned, the most lucrative investment that you can make throughout your working lifetime is your ability to earn an income—make it a priority to invest in your career. If you're fortunate enough to have the benefit of an employer savings program, then your investment potential is even greater. However, there is still a lot of confusion about employer-matching programs. Let's explore how to make the most of them. Once you understand your assets and how to manage them, you'll be ready to get the most out of your employee benefits.

Step #1: Learning about Assets

An asset is something that you own in your name and hope will increase in value over time, such as a house, piece of art, or a collector car. For the most part, investments are assets. There are three main asset classes, each of which carries different risks and potentials for return.

- Cash
- Fixed income/bonds
- Equity/stocks

Cash
Definition: This one is about as simple as it sounds: cash is the money in your wallet and safety deposit box, in a savings account, and in a term deposit at a bank or a money market mutual fund. A cash asset is an

investment that is easily accessible but for which you get a meager return because current interest rates are very low. The tradeoff is that your money is safe, liquid, and there are little to no fees to store it.

Return Opportunity: Little to no return on your investment. Your cash will barely beat out inflation when not invested elsewhere.

Bonds

Definition: As an investor, when you own a bond, you're *owed* money. The interest is fixed and is considered income that you're paid annually or more frequently, which is why this asset class is often referred to as *fixed income*. It's a relatively safe category of investments, but because your return is based on relatively low interest rates, the return opportunities are still low. A bond can be liquidated or sold on a bond market before it matures (unlike a Guaranteed Investment Certificate [GIC] at your bank).

A GIC is similar to a bond in many ways—it guarantees your investment and the interest rate over a set period of time, anywhere from one to five years, during which you cannot withdraw the funds unless you buy a redeemable GIC that pays an even lower rate of return. You're guaranteed to get back what you put in. You'll also have a more attractive interest rate than what you'd get at the bank for a similar type of investment, but your money is locked in for longer than any cash assets.

Return Opportunity: You'll see low to medium returns on bonds, depending on the security of the issuer. For example, the Bank of Canada is more secure than the City of Calgary, so they would offer less interest than the riskier municipality. A corporate bond is generally less secure, so it would likely have a higher rate of return.

Stocks

Definition: You can also purchase shares—or equity—to have partial ownership in a company in the form of stock. If the company does well, you do well, but if the company tanks or goes bankrupt, you could lose everything. If the company makes a nice profit, it can provide the shareholders (investors) with something called a *dividend*—a financial bonus for investing in the company.

If you have equity in a company, you own a part of it.

In Canada, if a company is public, the public can buy shares in it, and it's listed on the Toronto Stock Exchange. Nearly every country in the world has a stock exchange—a place where people can buy and sell shares of these companies. But no stock offers a guaranteed return, as stock prices fluctuate for a variety of reasons.

Return Opportunity: Stocks have an unlimited potential for return and unlimited risks as well.

Is a House an Investment?

Or is it an asset? For investment purposes, an investment is an asset that you hope will appreciate (go up in value) over time so that you can live off its profits when you sell it in retirement. Your house should not be considered an investment because you will still need a place to live, even in retirement. It is an asset because you hope it will appreciate over time, but it is not something you should consider as part of your retirement fund unless you plan on selling it at a significant profit to downsize to something much smaller.

What About Mutual Funds?

A mutual fund is a pool of investments that includes the professional services of a mutual fund manager. There are thousands of mutual funds available in the Canadian marketplace, which range in level of risk and opportunity for return.

A few things to note about mutual funds:

- They allow you to invest for a low buy-in. With some mutual funds, you can start investing with as little as $500, which you can contribute to monthly in increments as low as $25.
- They give you the ability to diversify your investments more than if you were buying individual securities—stocks, bonds, and cash-equivalent investments. For example, a balanced mutual fund might consist of some cash investments as well as a bundle of bonds and stocks. You can take advantage of what that fund owns for a fraction of the cost of buying the individual assets yourself.
- You can sell your mutual fund units on any business day.
- A professional money manager buys and sells assets in the fund on your behalf.
- There are a large range of options to choose from, such as:
  - Money market funds. These are safe and low risk, but provide low returns.
  - Bond funds.
  - Equity/stock funds.
  - Specialty funds that invest in sectors such as energy and tech, or that trade in foreign currencies, and so many more.

- There are multiple ways to buy mutual funds: at your bank, with your investment advisor or financial professional, as well as online.
- A criticism of mutual funds is their high management fees, which are outlined in the prospectus but are somewhat hidden in the fine print upon purchase. You may also have to pay a commission to the person selling you the fund.
- Index funds are a type of mutual fund that mirror what the stock market is doing—for better or worse. With no mutual fund manager deciding what to buy or sell on your behalf, the fees are considerably less.
- Exchange-Traded Funds (ETFs) are becoming increasingly popular because they allow you to invest in a certain market as a whole. In this case, there's no one picking this stock or that stock for you to hold—it's all the stocks in a given market (an index). With ETFs, you take the selection or human element out of the equation—your return is simply based on what the market (be it the Canadian stock market, a US or international market, or a submarket such as technology or energy) does as a whole. Similar to an index fund, if the market performs well, you profit; if the market performs poorly, you lose money. Again, without a manager actively buying and selling, the fees for ETFs are far less than a traditional mutual fund.
- If you have access to a group Registered Retirement Savings Plan (RRSP), you'll likely have a limited option of mutual funds available within your plan. The management fees are reduced compared to the cost of buying those same mutual funds within a personal RRSP (because of the buying power of the group).

Step #2: Understanding the Taxation of Assets

To fully understand both your employee financial benefits and your investments as a whole, it's important to understand the taxation of your assets. Let's imagine your assets are cars. When your cash, bond, and stock cars are sitting out on the street, they get taxed on what they earn every year or when you sell the asset—you may wish to shelter them from taxation by putting them in a garage.

When your cars (investments) are hanging out on the street, they have no protection.

Assume you had four different investments, one in each car. How much tax would you pay for every $100 earned?

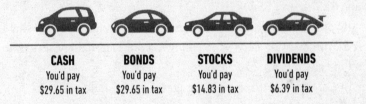

CASH	**BONDS**	**STOCKS**	**DIVIDENDS**
You'd pay	You'd pay	You'd pay	You'd pay
$29.65 in tax	$29.65 in tax	$14.83 in tax	$6.39 in tax

Let's assume that you earn a $50,000 salary and you live in Ontario just to give us a marginal tax bracket—your federal and provincial tax combined—to work within. If you invested money in each of the four investment types in a year and earned a $100 annual return in each, if you cashed out at the end of the year, the profit you'd walk away with would differ for each investment—you'll pay more taxes on certain investments for the same return. You pay the most in taxes when you get interest income from cash or a bond such as a Canadian government bond: to cash out $100 from either investment would cost you $29.65 in tax. You'll have to pay slightly less tax on stocks; to cash out $100 would cost you

$14.83 in taxes. Finally, you pay the least amount of taxes on dividends that result from preferred stocks that pay out in dividends: to cash out $100 would cost you $6.39 in taxes. This is called a qualified Canadian dividend.

It's more tax advantageous to have investments in stocks, because you will be taxed less every time you take money out of the investment or if it's sold. However, stocks and investments that provide dividends often involve more risk than investments that have higher tax rates. Taxation should, therefore, be only one factor when choosing your nonregistered investments, which are not protected by a tax shelter. If you see "nonregistered" on one of your investment statements, that's a clear indication that your cars are sitting on the street and not sheltered from taxes. A "registered" account would refer to an RRSP, group RRSP, Registered Retirement Income Fund (RRIF), Registered Education Savings Plan (RESP), or TFSA.

If your investments are in a Canadian tax shelter, they are sheltered from taxation each year. Following our car analogy, let's pretend tax shelters are like garages.

In Canada, the three main garages—or tax shelters—are:

- Registered Retirement Savings Plans (RRSP)
- Registered Education Savings Plans (RESP)
- Tax-Free Savings Accounts (TFSA)

With an RRSP and RESP, you defer paying taxes until you take the money out, which is beneficial because as long as your money stays in the plan you don't have to pay out yearly taxes. Your money is able to grow more quickly because of compound interest. If you invest $1,000 and earn 5 percent interest, that's an extra $50 in your plan. If you reinvest that $50, you're now earning 5 percent on the entire $1,050, and the cycle continues. It doesn't add up to much in the early years, but it will continue to snowball as you keep reinvesting your money.

With a TFSA, your money is truly tax-free: it can grow and be withdrawn tax free. The name "Tax-Free Savings Account" can be deceiving. Banks often advertise TFSAs as having low rates of return, and as a result, people mistakenly think TFSAs are not an attractive investment. What you have to remember is that a TFSA is like a garage—it's a tax shelter, not an actual investment. A TFSA, like an RRSP or an RESP, is the garage shielding your car from taxation. You can park a plethora of cars (investments) in each garage.

When your cars are parked in the garage (an RRSP, TFSA, or RESP) they have tax protection, special rules, and some perks.

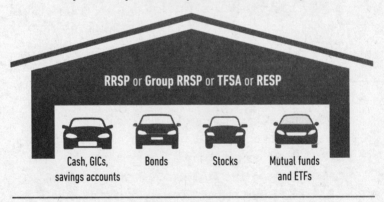

RRSP or Group RRSP or TFSA or RESP

Cash, GICs, savings accounts　　Bonds　　Stocks　　Mutual funds and ETFs

Each garage still needs cars—savings accounts, bonds, stocks, mutual funds, ETFs, etc.

Tell Me More

Tax Shelters

Here are some highlights of each tax shelter:

Registered Retirement Savings Plan (RRSP)

- You get a tax deduction when you invest in an RRSP that year. As your income increases, your marginal tax bracket (federal and provincial taxes) will increase, as will your annual tax refund.
- You can contribute up to 18 percent of your earned income (up to the maximum amount in any given year) from the previous year into your RRSP by March 1st of the following year. For example, if you had an earned income of $50,000 in 2018, you could invest $9,000 by March 1, 2019. If you don't have $9,000 to invest, you can defer investing, and that "room" you are entitled to each year would keep accumulating. Your Canada Revenue Agency notice of assessment lists how much unused room you have. Your 18 percent contribution applies to all of your RRSP accounts, so if you have a group RRSP through work as well as a personal RRSP, you can only contribute a total of $9,000 across both plans.
- The maximum you could contribute to your RRSP in 2018 was $26,230.
- An employer group RRSP may have extra restrictions that make it more difficult to withdraw money from your plan.
- The money in this garage grows tax deferred—you won't pay

any tax until you start withdrawing money, which usually happens at retirement. Ideally, by the time you use it, your income will be reduced, and you'll take the money out over a number of years or decades. This way, you only pay tax on what you take out each year.

- If you withdraw money from your RRSP while you're working, you'll be highly taxed based on your marginal tax bracket because your RRSP money is considered income.
- A major benefit of having an RRSP is that you get a tax deduction for the amount you contribute that year. Again, this is based on your marginal tax bracket.
- There are some special exceptions for when you can take money out of your RRSP without a tax hit: when you buy your first house or if you go back to school. However, you must pay that money back to your RRSP within a certain number of years or you'll be taxed on the withdrawal. Talk to your plan provider if you are looking to withdraw money from your RRSP for either reason.

Tax-Free Savings Account (TFSA)

- You can put money in and take money out at any time without paying any taxes. Your investments will grow tax free.
- You must be at least eighteen years old to open a TFSA.
- TFSAs first became available to Canadians in 2009 and originally had a contribution limit of $5,000 per year. The annual limit has fluctuated over the years, but currently it is $6,000.
- As with an RRSP, if you do not contribute your total yearly allowance, that "room" carries over each year. If you've never opened a TFSA and were eighteen years or older in 2009, you could contribute $63,500 in 2019.
- TFSAs also allow you to invest in a variety of things, including a savings account, bonds, stocks, mutual funds, exchange-traded funds (ETFs), and more. Many people confuse a TFSA

with an actual investment because "savings" is in the title. It's a tax shelter just like your RRSP and RESP, so you still need to choose the investments inside of it.

- There is not a tax refund with a TFSA because you're not taxed when you take the money out.

Registered Education Savings Plans (RESP)

- This plan is for saving for your child's education.
- There are individual and family RESPs. A family RESP allows more than one child to benefit from the plan.
- The money in this shelter grows tax deferred until you withdraw money from it. Ideally, when money comes out, you'll be using it for your child, who likely won't have much or any income, so they won't be highly taxed.
- The plan is set up under the adult's name, but the taxes are in the child's name once they use the money for educational expenses.
- There is no tax deduction with an RESP.
- The lifetime contribution limit is $50,000 per child.
- The biggest advantage of an RESP is that the Government of Canada matches 20 percent of your contributions per child per year through the Canadian Education Savings Grant (CESG). This matching program contributes the grant directly into your RESP account. Previously, the maximum CESG was $400 per child per year, but in the 2007 federal budget, the limit was increased to $500, with a lifetime maximum per child of $7,200. Lower income families are eligible to receive slightly higher CESGs and may also be eligible for the Canada Learning Bond.

Step #3: Ask the Right Questions

To fully understand what is available to you, meet with your human resources department, attend an employee session put on by your pension or group RRSP administrators if they're available, or call the toll-free number on any of your plan statements to get more information.

Don't be intimidated if the information is overwhelming or confusing. Learning something new can seem daunting. As you do your research, ask more questions, and become part of the process, you'll gain the knowledge you need to succeed. If you have a unique pension, are leaving your employer, or have questions that are beyond your available resources, consider hiring a fee-only Certified Financial Planner who can walk you through your benefits and options.

Step #4: Max Out Your Matching Potential

If your employer offers a matching program, try to contribute the maximum amount that they'll match. If you can't make it work in your budget, try to reassess how and where you're spending money to see if you can reconfigure. Take a look at the Thirty-Day Anti-Budget in chapter 4: you might just be able to find the money. Employer-matching programs essentially offer free money that you otherwise wouldn't have access to. Take advantage of it.

Step #5: Don't Touch Your RRSP until Retirement

Do not use your RRSP as an emergency fund, and do not take money out of it before retirement. An emergency fund should have three to six months' worth of your salary and should be in a liquid account, and dipping into your RRSP should be your last resort.

Not only will you be taxed fully the year you withdraw the money, but you'll also never be able to get that room back on your plan. Thankfully, this doesn't apply to the Home Buyers' Plan or when using your RRSP for eligible post-secondary education.

Step #6: Ask for What You Deserve

In order to maximize your potential earnings, negotiate your starting salary—you don't have to simply agree to the first number they give you. Once you've been an employee for a while and you think you've earned it, ask for regular raises. If you work for an organization that publicizes the salary range for your position, you can still ask for more if your skills and experience justify it. When it comes to your salary, you don't know if you don't ask.

If an increase in salary isn't negotiable, you have other options: you can request a better office, a new job title, more vacation time, or flexible hours, to name a few. If you're new to negotiating or you're intimidated by the task, start small. Can you get a discount or upgrade while travelling? Can you get last week's sale price even though the sale has expired? You won't always get a yes, but if nothing else, it will demonstrate that you're looking for unique forms of praise or recognition of your contributions.

If you're uncomfortable with negotiating, you're not alone. If you think negotiating is rude and pushy, or only a necessity for lower-income families, that's simply not the case. You just have to change your perception.

Growing up in a household where money was always tight, I used to hate how closely my mom would watch the till when we were buying groceries. Eventually I learned that she had to. She used cash in those days, so if we didn't keep a mental tally of our groceries as we shopped, we faced the embarrassment of having to put items back if she didn't have enough. Even as my mom shopped for larger items like a new washing machine or refrigerator, she would always try to get a better deal, even if there was already a sale. I found the entire process humiliating and felt like we had a big flashing neon sign above our heads that read "poor."

As a young adult, I never haggled, asked for a better deal, or even checked over my bills to ensure I wasn't being overcharged. It wasn't until I was in the financial industry and I witnessed my clients paying close attention to every dollar they spent, even though they were financially stable, that I reevaluated my position. My clients were proud of getting a better deal for themselves. Now I see that my mom was proud of getting better deals as well. I just didn't appreciate her skills at the time.

Salary negotiation has the potential to have a big impact on your life, so it's important to at least try. Practice your requests aloud with a friend or to yourself before actually having the conversation with your boss. If the answer is no, take it as an opportunity to find out what you need to do to continue to grow and prosper within the company.

Step #7: Check Your Beneficiaries

Your beneficiaries will receive your assets when you pass away, and you'll be asked to name your beneficiaries on a variety of forms beyond your will, including but not limited to: your life and disability policies, pension, group RRSP, individual RRSP, and RESPs. Check that your forms are consistent across all plans and within your will.

Step #8: Get Your Blind Spots Checked

You may have life and disability insurance through work, but is it enough to cover your liabilities? Do you need extra protection from a critical illness policy that would pay out a lump sum amount in the event of a major life illness like a heart attack or cancer? Do you have a current will, power of attorney, and living will? Most of these documents are inexpensive and relatively easy to have drafted, but they can bring up difficult topics that might seem hard to address. You likely don't want to have to think about your death or possible disability, but addressing these issues and ensuring that your documents are up-to-date can benefit your loved ones in the future—you will avoid confusion and save money by planning ahead. A Certified Financial Planner, lawyer, or Chartered Professional Accountant can help you get your money matters and documents straightened out.

Step #9: Don't Forget about Your Investments

The first step is making the initial investment. The second step is keeping an eye on them. You get a metaphorical gold star for maxing out your employer's matching program through a group RRSP, but you'll also want to review your investments each year to ensure that they still suit your needs and are balanced with any investments you have at other financial institutions. As your money grows, you'll need to make adjustments to meet any increasing need for professional investment and retirement planning. At this point, I'd suggest interviewing appropriate advisors or financial planners for your unique situation.

Shopping for a Financial Advisor

If you're making investments, you may wish to hire someone who provides advice and sells investment products specifically, such as a financial advisor, investment advisor, wealth manager, or a mutual fund salesperson. Frustratingly, their title doesn't mean much. Even if they hold a designation such as a Certified Financial Planner (CFP) or

Chartered Financial Analyst (CFA), you'll want to do your homework to ensure they're licensed and the right fit for you. Here are some questions you'll want to ask before hiring a professional:

- What are you licensed to sell?
- What regulatory body are you registered with?
- What fees do you charge and how are they charged? Annual fees, commissions, per-transaction, or trade fees?
- Will they provide all recommendations in writing?
- What products or services are they not licensed to sell? This will give you an idea of their biases—if they're only licensed to sell life insurance products, it's unlikely they're going to recommend a stock or exchange-traded fund (ETF).

Once you've done your homework, ask for references, do a Google search, and check with the federal regulator in Canada, the Canadian Securities Administrators, as well as your provincial regulators, such as the Alberta Securities Commission or the Ontario Securities Commission. You'll want to check that their registration is valid, that they aren't already flagged on a watch list, and that their license or designation is in good standing.

Step #10: Make Your Career Your Fourth Asset Class

You now know about the three main asset classes—cash, bonds/fixed income, and stocks/equity—but your career should also be seen as an asset. For example, while a teacher may have high job stability, they may be more conservative with their investments. However, if a teacher treated their career as a fourth asset class and recognized that their job is relatively low risk, they could take a little more risk with their investments. Conversely, an entrepreneur with a high-risk job with a possibly fluctuating income might embrace taking risks and, therefore, may make riskier investments. However, because their career asset is already carrying so much risk, an entrepreneur might want to be a bit more cautious with their investments. Consider your career—and that of your spouse—a fourth asset when determining how to spread out the risk of your investments.

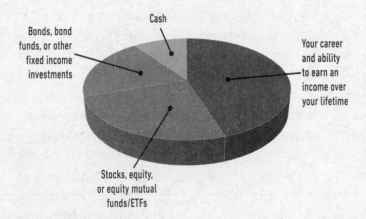

Cash

Bonds, bond funds, or other fixed income investments

Your career and ability to earn an income over your lifetime

Stocks, equity, or equity mutual funds/ETFs

This is a sample of how your overall asset allocation—or diversification—might look like when you factor in your career.

Step #11: Choose Well-Rounded Investments

When you're making investment choices, don't put all your eggs in one basket, especially if you have a group RRSP on top of other individual investment plans. It can become more difficult to see the full picture of all your diversified investments, while still keeping your goals in mind, when they're spread out. We are all living busy lives, and many of us have a full-time job that does not involve researching our investment potential. To save time, the average person must rely on the wisdom of diversification.

To ensure your investments are well rounded, you need to think about negative correlation—it sounds complex, but it's quite simple. No matter what is happening with the economy, interest rates, or the stock market, you want to ensure that your investments aren't all performing uniformly. Your investments shouldn't be all going up or all going down.

Let's think about the negative correlation of investment opportunities at a beach resort. You can invest in the suntan lotion company, the umbrella company, or a hotdog stand. If you invest in the suntan lotion company, your investment will succeed based on the number of sunny days in a year. If you invest in the umbrella company, your investment's success will depend on the number of rainy days in that year. Which would you choose? Since it's never sunny while it's raining, an elegant solution would be to invest in both. That's how you can negatively correlate your portfolio and reduce your investment risk—invest in options that don't go up and down according to the same criteria.

Alternatively, the hotdog stand is not the most lucrative option, but the success is dependable because beachgoers are hungry, rain or shine. The hotdog stand is like your "cash" asset class—it never returns much, but it's a stable bet, and almost every investment portfolio should have some cash reserves.

WHERE ARE THEY NOW?

Lyndsay was ready to ask for a raise at work but didn't want to face rejection. To prepare herself, she went for lunch with her aunt, a successful executive, who provided some much-needed guidance on the "ask." She suggested that Lyndsay set up a meeting with her boss not to demand a raise, but to briefly overview three of her shining achievements as a way of leading into a conversation about what's possible for advancement in her near future—with her overall position, title, and salary.

The meeting was a great success. Lyndsay found out that her

boss was super-stressed with his own work challenges and didn't realize that she was ready to advance in her career. He outlined a few things for her to work on, and before the end of the conversation, she asked to book a follow-up meeting with him in three months. Just a few months after the initial meeting, Lyndsay received an extra week of holiday pay and a 2.5 percent annual salary increase. With her confidence renewed, she asked for a second follow-up meeting in six months to discuss more responsibilities and a possible second raise, to which her boss agreed. She's looking forward to bringing her A-game over the coming months and will be documenting her achievements throughout to present to him when they meet again.

Both Terrance and Lyndsay dug into their employer's benefits and found that they were not taking full advantage of all of their financial opportunities. It didn't seem like much per year ($800 for Terrance and $1,200 for Lyndsay), but they knew that their money would grow over the course of their working career if they stayed with the same employers. They both attended their company info sessions to discover their investment options inside of their respective group RRSPs and learned that their contributions had been sitting in cash investments. While cash investments are super-safe, Terrance and Lyndsay can afford to choose riskier investments because they have years before they'll need their money. They've replaced cash with the "balanced fund" option (a mix of bonds, stocks, and some cash) because they have lots of time to earn gradually on their way to retirement. They want to ease into taking a little more risk but feel great that their money is being put to better use within the plan. They've also found enough money to maximize their contributions to their employer's matching program by packing their lunches at home to cut out the cost of expensive restaurant bills. They feel like they've taken the ultimate adulting course and have passed with flying colours. Now, they just need to keep up the great work, and maximize their options each year.

All Show

Have you been out to a restaurant lately? Did anyone at the table take a photo of their meal or their drink? It's become a new norm, as people feel the need to share that *they* too can have nice things—whether that be the newest phone, a four-star meal, or a trip to a luxury resort. The problem is that we *can't* always afford to keep up with each other. And although it gets expensive, some people will go out of their way to prove to the world that they are richer than you think (even if they really aren't).

Marcus didn't grow up with a lot, and he hoped he'd never have to feel poor once he was making his own money. His mom stayed home and took care of her six children while his dad worked for the railroad. It was a good job with benefits and steady pay, but it never seemed to be enough to cover the things Marcus and his siblings so desperately wanted. Even though he knew his parents worked hard to provide for the family, Marcus still felt ashamed and inadequate in comparison to his friends.

After living through poverty, Marcus was inspired to work

in the not-for-profit sector to help families like his own who are struggling to make ends meet. He loves his work, but with a salary of only $50,000, Marcus lives paycheque to paycheque and many of his friends make double his salary. By the time he's covered his rent, his elite gym membership, after-work drinks, and weekly Sunday brunch, Marcus hardly has enough money to buy groceries or pay his bills at the end of the month. His credit card has become his "best friend" as he struggles to find the money necessary to keep up with his friends. He loves his job, is passionate about the work he does, and doesn't want to leave his position for a higher salary. He doesn't know how much longer he'll be able to straddle both worlds.

WHERE HE WENT WRONG

Marcus is constantly comparing himself to his peers and spends more money than he makes to keep up the illusion that he's richer than he is. After growing up with so little, Marcus often spends money on himself to feel rich. If he doesn't address the underlying feelings of scarcity and inadequacy, and connect with what really matters, he'll be playing catch-up for the rest of his life.

Misstep #1: Compare and Contrast

How often are you comparing yourself to others? Every week? Every day? Whatever the case, you're not alone. It's hard not to compare ourselves to every highly filtered Instagram post we see and then feel like a failure in our own life. But think about it for a moment. How many times have you posted something online that wasn't a true depiction of your own experience? Maybe you fought with your spouse all throughout dinner but still spent half an hour posting a perfectly filtered photo of your meal before eating it? Whether it's conscious or not, you want your friends to envy your experience. Even if the reality sucked.

For many generations, wealth was very visible—you could guess someone's economic status through their clothing, housing, and general appearance. Today, with the popularity of credit and low interest rates (for mortgages and lines of credit), people can look like a million bucks even when swimming in debt. Marcus is heading in that direction. As he compares himself to his friends, he has no idea how they manage it. It's possible they can afford it, but it's also more likely that they're using credit to fund their lavish lifestyles. No doubt, they're putting off saving, or they're living off gifts from their parents.

Unless you're reading someone's net worth statement, you have no idea if their outward appearance matches their financial status. Marcus needs to start evaluating his worth based on his own success and accomplishments, not in relation to other people's finances.

Misstep #2: Financial Hangover

Thirty years ago, interest rates for a mortgage or loan were in the high double digits, so people were less likely to borrow money that they couldn't afford. Unfortunately, with today's interest rates Marcus can rely on his borrowing power and has convinced himself that he can afford to live up to his friends' lavish standards. Now, with interest rates at a historical low, we've become accustomed to debt and using "cheap" credit to fund our lifestyles. The government has encouraged this because it stimulates the economy, creates jobs, and increases bank profits. However, it's terrible for our bottom line. Borrowing can be a wise and a prudent strategy when all the risks are considered, but willingly taking on debt merely for consumption purposes can create a financial hangover that you'll be paying off for years to come.

Do you remember that *Seinfeld* bit where Jerry and his friends arrive at a restaurant famished? They order an appetizer, a side dish, and several main courses, and eat to the point of being stuffed. When the bill arrives, Jerry is shocked as he reads through all the items and exclaims, "Who ordered all this food?" Now that his hunger has passed, he has to pay for the cost of needing instant gratification without having considered the financial consequences. When you use debt to buy things now, you'll be paying for it for years to come.

Misstep #3: Now or Never

Marcus, along with many of his generation, watched his parents and grandparents work too hard and live frugally their entire lives to the point that they never had the time to enjoy their money. Now Marcus has vowed to enjoy his life and his money while he can. To an extent, there's nothing wrong with that. As they say, you can't take it with you. However, you also need to be realistic about what you can afford. While older generations (the baby boomers' parents, for example) saved toward a goal of buying a house in their fifties or sixties, now twentysomethings lament that they can't afford a house *immediately*. Similarly, Marcus's parents took him and his siblings on a family vacation just twice in their lifetime; meanwhile, he expects to go on a great vacation every year! Living and funding your dream life today will leave nothing for your future self.

Is this something you've noticed yourself doing too? Remember, it's not always possible to meet every desire now, but think of how satisfying it would feel to take the time to save up and really earn it.

Misstep #4: Keeping Up with the Joneses

No, not the 2016 spy film starring Jon Hamm and Gal Gadot as Mr. and Mrs. Jones. I mean the idiom used in reference to the effect of comparing yourself to your peers as a means of measuring your social success and standing. Researchers have gone so far as to quantify it by studying lottery winners and the effect the winnings had on surrounding neighbours, and the results were shocking. For every $1,000 that your neighbour wins in the lottery, your chance of going bankrupt increases by 2.4 percent.[12] The good news is that the odds that your neighbour will win the lottery are still slim.

How can someone else's good fortune increase your financial demise? Well, it's the result of keeping up with the Joneses! As you watch your newly wealthy neighbour accumulate new things and go on outings, the research shows that you'll want and expect those things for yourself, and you will go into debt to make it happen. The trick is to recognize the effect others have on you and your purchasing habits in an effort to combat it. Once you're aware that this flaw exists in the pleasure centers of our brains, you can work to resist it by sticking to your financial plan.

Marcus's aspirational friends can help him set lofty goals that stretch his thinking, but he has to keep in mind that he doesn't earn as much as his friends. It's okay to bow out of activities that are beyond your means—or come up with suggestions for outings that are easy on the wallet.

Misstep #5: Spending It All

If Marcus doesn't start saving a portion of his income regardless of what he's making, he's unlikely to ever develop crucial savings habits. If you can't save 10 percent of your salary when you're only making $40,000, it's unlikely you'll do it even if you're making $150,000. As your income increases, so do your expenses. Making a habit of saving a percentage of each paycheque will ensure you're always saving an appropriately proportionate amount.

When I was working in the financial industry, I'd often meet millionaires who'd saved their way there—they had started out with modest careers as teachers, drivers, and tradespeople. Of course, I'd also advise rich lawyers, surgeons, and celebrities, but you'd be surprised by how many wealthy people don't keep track of their money—until it's gone. It's not just about how much you make. It's what you do with it that counts. Spend some, save some. It's a balancing game. The trick to winning is consistently setting aside a percentage of your salary. Start with 10 percent, if you can, and work to increase that percentage as you go.

Mistake #6: Falling for "Get Rich Quick" Schemes

Marcus wants to start investing, even though he doesn't have anything to invest yet. Some of his friends brag about the incredible returns they're getting with cryptocurrencies and second mortgage investments. He's tempted by these lucrative opportunities, but with no investment experience, he doesn't understand that these high-risk investments can be as volatile and unpredictable as hoping to profit by playing poker or the slots at a casino.

If you don't have the money to invest right now, that's okay. Give yourself time. Don't go into debt for the sake of investing. That might sound like common sense, but a study recently found that in the US, one in five students are actually using their student loan funds to invest in the very high-risk game of cryptocurrencies.[13] Be wary of these get-rich schemes. Sometimes you win, but most of the time you don't. Even if you are constantly hearing about how successful someone has been in investing in one of these schemes, remember that people are less likely to share about their losses. You only hear about the wins.

THE SOLUTION?

Marcus can reassess his spending and saving habits without changing his job or his group of peers. If you see yourself making some of the same financial decisions as Marcus, here's how you can redirect your habits.

Step #1: Expand Your Horizons

A little variety is a good thing, even when it comes to your peers. No, don't go abandoning friends simply because you don't make the same salary. Rather, I'm suggesting that if you find yourself having to dip into your savings or rely on credit to afford hanging out with your friends, then maybe you should expand your options.

Marcus made most of his friends at school, many of whom went on to high-paying corporate jobs, while he transitioned into the not-for-profit sector. As he continues to network and bridge the gap between work friends and real friends, Marcus will start to see that he doesn't have to spend a lot of money to find value and meaning in life. It's amazing what a fresh perspective can do for your wallet.

I learned this lesson the hard way. I, like Marcus, grew up in a household with a tight budget, so in my early twenties I was showy with my money in an effort to keep up with my wealthy clients. At twenty-three years old, my boyfriend at the time convinced me to buy a brand-new Mercedes sedan. I loved that car for the first few months, but I decimated my emergency savings for the down payment, and the monthly lease payment gobbled up every free cent I

had. Not to mention the mandatory cost of the regular car servicing, where each visit cost more than my monthly lease payment. I
liked that car less and less, to the point of resenting every time I
had to get in it.

I made the most of my money by seeing the lease through, at
which point I bought it out. I kept my Mercedes for over thirteen
years, until it started to fall apart. When it was time to buy a new
car, I defaulted to shopping for a new high-end brand because all
my friends had luxury cars. I was blown away by how much cars
had increased in price and decreased in roominess, but I had nonetheless been sold on buying a Lexus. But it didn't feel quite right—
the car was nearly twice the cost of my first condo, and I didn't
even really like it. I only thought I should have it because it would
help me fit in with my friends.

Thankfully, a new friend (along with my fiscally responsible
husband) interrupted my unconscious buying pattern. On the day
I was going to buy the Lexus, I bumped into my friend and mentioned I was on my way to buy the car but that I was uncomfortable with the price. In response, he quipped that if I bought a fully
loaded, full-sized Hyundai, I could still get a beautiful car and use
the leftover money to fix the eyes of thousands of people in devel-
oping countries who were going blind. You see, this friend of mine
volunteers as a skilled eye surgeon with Doctors Without Borders
around the world. He wasn't trying to guilt me or sway my decision
in any way, but in his world a luxury car didn't have more value
than a perfectly good car that cost three times less.

With this new perspective in mind, I visited a Hyundai showroom, where I immediately spotted a decked-out, full-sized sedan,
complete with a sports package. The car was stunning and just
what we needed—we still have it to this day. Unfortunately, when
my husband and I showed up in my new car to meet a bunch of
friends at our monthly dinner club a few weeks later, we were met

by looks of shock. During dinner, they asked my husband if business was going well, thinking we had suffered a setback. Why else would I downgrade? I had to make a conscious effort to not be bothered by their opinions, but I love the car, the savings, and the fact that I chose value over appearances.

Step #2: Check Your Neurons

There's a reason why we want to spend when we see others doing so, why we have FOMO, and why we are all trying to keep up with the Joneses. Call it faulty wiring or evolution or a marketer's dream come true. Whatever you want to call it, the truth is that your brain responds to the actions of those around you. Have you ever gone from full to starving in the span of sixty seconds while watching TV? It's amazing how appetizing they can make a pizza look in a commercial. This is the result of mirror neurons in your brain.

Years ago, researchers discovered mirror neurons—a pleasure region in the brains of monkeys. It would light up when the monkey observed a researcher licking an ice cream cone, as if the monkey itself were enjoying the ice cream. Advertisers and YouTubers have taken advantage of this effect, especially through the recent phenomenon of unboxing videos—there's a satisfaction in watching others experience the things we want. The problem is when we're influenced into wanting something that we otherwise would not have known or cared about.

When you see someone sporting a fancy pair of shoes, driving a shiny new car, or posting pictures of a Caribbean getaway, your brain responds and initiates a desire for the experience. There are actions you can take to combat this. Start by being aware of how your mirror neurons might be affecting your purchasing habits. Creating distance by being consciously aware of external influences will arm you with a sense of ease and validation that your willpower isn't faulty. You can blame your brain simply for being wired for pleasure, instant gratification, and coveting what others have. And you can reassure yourself that you're actually just fine with what you already have. Bring on the gratitude, and resist the instant gratification.

Step #3: Create a Thirty-Day Anti-Budget

If you have a budget and actually stick to it, then you can happily skip this step. If you're still reading, you're not alone. Budgets simply don't work for everyone. They're like diets: restrictive, punitive, and tough to figure out how to start, even if they make an impact in the long run. So how can you stick to a budget of $250 for groceries and dining out if you're consistently spending $450 a month? It's not sustainable and will likely result in shame, guilt, and abandoning the budget.

Don't despair! With an anti-budget you track your spending for thirty days to discover how you are using your money. You'll be set up for success as you become mindful and aware of your spending habits. The anti-budget is an exercise in awareness and behavioural changes. I make a point of repeating this exercise every six months, and I suggest you do the same.

Thirty-Day Anti-Budget

There are four rules:

One: Track

Track all of your spending for thirty days. It sounds simple in theory, but you'll probably find that it's harder in practice. You can go old-school with a tracking book, which you can usually find at the dollar store. The idea is to write down every dollar you spend over the course of a month. After just a week, you should notice a difference in how mindful you are about spending. It's become too easy to be numb to spending—we just tap and go, rarely taking the time to savour our purchases or recognize how we're spending our money.

If you want to track digitally, you can do so easily with a spreadsheet or through your bank if you rely on one credit and debit card. Check online with your bank to see what tracking options they offer. If you don't want to keep track of your spending on a daily basis, you can also comb through your statements at the end of the month.

For this exercise, think of yourself as a financial detective as you look beyond your thirty-day spending habits. What interest costs are you paying for any loans, credit cards, or mortgage payments? How much do you spend annually on your income taxes? Did you incur any bank fees, nonsufficient funds (NSF) charges, or other overage fees? Remember to include all costs associated with subscriptions, insurance, investments, and anything else you can find.

Two: Categorize

At the end of the month, categorize your spending. Here are some of the common categories I use for the exercise:

- Dining out
- Groceries
- Transportation
- Housing
- Entertainment
- Alcohol
- Gifts

Be as specific and detailed as you can. Calculate the amount of money you spent in each category.

Three: Multiply by Twelve

Take the amount you spent in a thirty-day period in each category, and multiply those totals by twelve. This is an estimate of how much money you'll spend in each category across an entire year if you continue to follow the same spending habits. How do you feel after seeing the costs for a full year?

Four: Determine Where You Want Your Money to Go

Are there any categories in which you're spending money that could be reduced, negotiated, or eliminated? You'd be amazed by how much money you can save by negotiating with your various providers for things such as your cell phone, cable, internet plans, and even the interest on your credit cards. What are you and your family willing to part with? It's not about sacrifice, but rather it's about choice and awareness. If you spend a lot on dining out but it's an important part of your social life, that's fine! Are there other choices or adjustments you can make? Maybe if you're out all the time, you don't still need your cable or subscription magazines.

A friend of mine did the Thirty-Day Anti-Budget, and discovered that he was spending $3,500 a year on Diet Coke alone—a bad habit *and* a waste of money! He replaced his Diet Coke purchases with a SodaStream for under $200 and is feeling healthier already. Another said that he and his wife were certain that they had zero room to cut any spending, but after completing the anti-budget, they vowed to put a toonie in a jar every time one of them went out for breakfast, lunch, dinner, or coffee. After only a year, they'd put aside nearly a thousand dollars in toonies. Maybe you really are richer than you think.

That's it—four simple steps! The last time I did my Thirty-Day Anti-Budget, I noticed that I was spending $100 a month on bottled water whenever I was travelling for business. That's $1,200 a year! I invested in a reusable bottle, and now I'm cutting down on both my ecological footprint and my annual spending. In past years, my husband and I have discovered that we were wasting money on magazines and other subscriptions that we didn't have time to actually use. When you look at what those wasted dollars represent annually, it's hard not to want to reassess where your money is going.

Step #4: Find More Money

In personal finance, we too often only look at ways to cut expenses, and we can forget that there's another side to the ledger: bringing in more money! There are a number of ways you and your family can expand your income. Off the top of my head, here are a few ideas to get your own brainstorming session started:

- If you have teenage children, encourage them to use money from part-time jobs or their own savings for certain extra expenses. Engaging teens with family finances is always a good thing, because money doesn't grow on trees!
- Can you buy and resell items online?
- Do you have a skill that you can teach like tutoring, musical lessons, or cooking classes?
- Would you consider taking advantage of online services such as Airbnb, Uber, or Fiverr to bring in extra income?

Step #5: Get Creative with Expenses

It's likely that you currently have expenses that you could reduce or eliminate by thinking creatively about how to enjoy the same experiences with little to no costs. What skills or resources can you put to use that will offset the costs of things you are already paying for? Again, to help spark ideas, here's a small list of suggestions:

- Can you use technical or artistic skills to help create branding or a website for a local restaurant in exchange for free meals for a month?
- Does the new gym in your neighbourhood need someone with your social media skills to spruce up their accounts in exchange for a membership?

- If you love going to concerts, art galleries, and festivals, can you volunteer your time at events or venues to both give back to your community and enjoy the experience at the same time?

Step #6: Volunteer

If you're hoping to upgrade or gain new skills and abilities but the cost of enrolling in classes is beyond your means, consider volunteering your time with organizations that align with your interests and goals. You'll build new skill sets and network with a group of people who might help you further your career and offer new opportunities down the line. Over the years, I've learned a lot about fundraising, governance, and marketing just from participating on various committees. And it didn't cost me a penny.

Step #7: Protect Your Money

As you start saving money to put toward your emergency account and nest egg, it's important to take into account how you will protect it. Why does your money need protection? Because investments involve risk, and with risk comes the possibility of losing your money. If you have time on your side—if you're beginning your career and won't need your money until retirement—you can take on more risk. If you do suffer any losses, you'll have time to recoup it. In theory, the rise and fall of a riskier investment will balance out over a longer period. Remember, though, that a dollar lost hurts much more than the potential to make two dollars.

As Marcus struggles to save any money, he is making the costly mistake of hearing and believing the success stories of his friends' financially risky investments without truly understanding how they work. Just as you shouldn't compare your success to others, you also shouldn't compare your investment performance to that of your peers. As we've discussed, most people only talk about their investments when they are profiting and will otherwise omit the details when they are losing. It's not effective to rely on the advice or choices of your friends. You wouldn't want to build a nest egg only to then watch it disappear through bad investment choices or sit stagnant in the wrong account or investment, or lose money to unnecessary fees and taxes. It's your money—you choose what to do with it and how to protect it.

When you're ready to grow your savings, learn about what you're investing in, seek the advice of a professional, and don't listen to the unsolicited advice made by people who might not understand what they're talking about.

Step #8: Connect with Your Future Self

Let's do an exercise together. Think about yourself for a moment—parts of your medial prefrontal cortex just lit up. Now, think of a stranger—that part of your brain just dimmed. If you try to think of yourself in ten or twenty years, that same part of your medial prefrontal cortex will remain unlit. You are wired not to be invested in your future self, because your brain thinks of that person as a stranger. And why would you want to save for a stranger?

Would you give your morning latte or new purse to a stranger on the subway? Likely not. So why would you delay the gratification of having what you want today for a stranger in the future? To do so, you must build a relationship with the person you will become so you can save for that eventuality. The more you connect with your future self, the more you'll feel compelled to delay some of that instant gratification.

To maintain an ongoing relationship with your future self, do this exercise once a week for thirty days. Just as with your Thirty-Day Anti-Budget, do the following exercise once every six months. Provide as many details as possible, but feel free to start with broad ideas if the future seems too fuzzy at first.

- In ten years:
  - *How old will you be?*
  - *What will you be doing?*
  - *Who will you be spending your time with?*
  - *What does your life look like?*
- In twenty years:
  - *How old will you be?*
  - *What does your life look like?*
  - *What do you want to be doing?*
  - *Where do you want to be?*
- Approximately how much money will it take you to reach the goals you've set for yourself ten years and twenty years from now?
- On a scale from one to ten, how do you rank your relationship to money when it comes to your:
  - *Skills:* _____
  - *Interest:* _____
  - *Time:* _____

Now that you've taken the time to think it through, list one thing that you're willing to do in the next thirty days that will help your future self financially. Here are a few suggestions: phone your pension plan provider, learn how to negotiate, get a financial professional, see a nonprofit credit counsellor, or track your spending for thirty days.

Step #9: Get Help to Create a Plan

If you're reading this book, chances are that you're ready to make a change for the better, but you need a plan to get you there. You already know that I love the definition of insanity as doing the same thing repeatedly and expecting a different result, so making a change is the first step to improvement. There are small changes you can make, such as using online calculators to see where you stand financially, taking a finance class, or expanding your financial literacy by reading the personal finance and investing sections of your favourite news source.

Beyond these small changes, you may need to seek help from a professional such as a Certified Financial Planner, nonprofit credit counsellor, or Chartered Professional Accountant, who can help you make a plan with your money blind spots in mind.

Positive Peer Effects

New research suggests that when you or someone close to you changes their behaviour for better or worse, it changes the behaviours of the group. If you start running, smoking, or bingeing, your friends and family can be affected. Even if they don't live in the same city. As you improve your financial life, whether you realize it or not, you're helping those around you possibly make positive money changes too. Also, as you become more honest about your financial limitations, others around you will feel better fessing up to their own. That deserves a pat on the back!

WHERE IS HE NOW?

After doing the Thirty-Day Anti-Budget, Marcus was blown away by tracking and tallying his spending. Three categories really opened his eyes:

1. Going out for drinks three times a week with buddies added up to $360/month, or $4,320/year.
2. His weekly brunch with friends was setting him back $160/month, or $1,920/year.
3. His fancy gym membership cost him $1,800 a year.

When he saw the annual amounts clearly laid out, Marcus understood how he was stuck living financially stretched every month.

He decided to cut down his social drinks to once a week and would limit brunch to every other Sunday. After saving that money over a few months, Marcus was able to spend $400 on some weights and used gym equipment so he could work out at home. He cancelled his gym membership. He also joined a free running group twice a week that easily replaced his drinking time with friends. This new group is much more concerned with health than their fancy toys, and it's been refreshing to hang out with people who share different values.

To further broaden his horizons, Marcus started volunteering for his local Chamber of Commerce in hopes of meeting some successful businesspeople to learn from. He's attending all of their networking events for free as a volunteer, and he has been invited to sit on one of their committees. He's meeting leaders of the community he would never otherwise have had access to.

At the suggestion of a successful businesswoman, Marcus started a mastermind group to meet with other like-minded people in his industry. He gathered a list of thirty people to invite, many of whom he'd met from volunteering for the chamber and had kept in touch with on LinkedIn. Eight people agreed to join the group, and they meet once a month at a restaurant or library and share their successes, challenges, and resources as a group. Marcus has learned so much from this diverse group of achievement-focused business owners and entrepreneurs, and their meetings have sparked so many ideas for him. Since he's cut back on his weekly brunches, he spends two Sundays a month scouring antique and thrift stores for treasures to resell online. After some research on pricing, he resells his finds on eBay, Facebook Marketplace, and online classified services.

Over the last year, Marcus has cut back his expenses, found supportive new peer groups, and developed a fun, flourishing side gig. As a result, he has fully paid off one of his credit cards with the other close behind. Plus, he has a few thousand dollars sitting in the bank. He loves the feeling of not living paycheque to paycheque, and as he looks back on the year and his life and money modifications, he feels proud of himself and his prospects for the future.

5

The Car Trap

Public transit can only take you so far. It's a great way to save on the countless bills associated with owning a car, but as your life—and perhaps your family—expands, a car might become a necessary evil. But everyone's heard that a car loses value the minute you drive it off the lot, so how will you decide how to spend your hard-earned money on a decidedly bad investment?

Dave and Melissa learned how not to buy a car the hard way, when they moved to a suburban neighbourhood in Calgary and were embarrassed by how much their van and compact car stood out on the street. Everyone had a shiny new truck or SUV, an apparent necessity in the prairie winters—"Think of the twins' safety!" was enough to convince them. Melissa and Dave were exhausted from the move, overwhelmed with getting the kids in their new school, adjusting to a new life, trying to make friends at work and at home, but they decided to shop for a new car.

They had no idea what make, model, or vehicle they were looking for, but they wanted this project ticked off their long to-do list. The twins were agitated, Melissa and Dave hadn't eaten since breakfast, and there were endless options in the showroom and out on the massive parking lot. As the hot sun beat down, the sales guy approached with ice-cold bottles of water and pretzels for the kids—it was love at first sight!

Michael, a friendly face in the sea of car options, immediately narrowed their choices with two easy questions, "What are you going to use the vehicle for, *and* how much can you afford?" With such an easy introduction, Melissa and Dave both breathed a sigh of relief. Best choice ever to stop at this dealership—the first and last stop! After only fifteen minutes, Michael had selected the make, model, and size of an SUV for both Melissa and Dave.

In less than an hour, Melissa and Dave had signed countless documents for extras like undercarriage protection, loan protection, disability protection, and other admin fees. Even though they couldn't afford the cars, they agreed to use their emergency account to help pay the down payment and make the monthly financing work. Michael also persuaded them to trade in their current cars to get a better deal. They hadn't negotiated any of the fees, but they didn't care. They were walking out of the dealership as the owners of two new SUVs!

Break It Down

A car is the second-largest purchase you'll ever make in your life, and you're likely to make it many times over. Yet, unlike the home-buying process where you might have the professional assistance of a Realtor, mortgage broker, lawyer, and Certified Financial Planner, Canadians often handle the car-buying process alone—and not very well.

Here's a breakdown of the cost of Melissa and Dave's decision:

	Melissa's SUV	Dave's SUV	Notes
Down payment	$10,000	$10,000	They both put $10,000 down, and only at the end of signing the financing papers did Michael say that the monthly amount would be "slightly more" than the $600 they had budgeted.
Monthly financing cost	$650 a month for 6 years	$625 a month for 5.5 years	
Subtotal	$46,800	$41,250	They both bought similar SUVs, but Melissa's was a bit more expensive.
Total	$88,050		Decided upon in under two hours.

WHERE THEY WENT WRONG

Let's dissect where Melissa and Dave went wrong and how you can avoid making the same mistakes. You'll see that if you plan ahead and do your research, like with anything else in life, you'll almost always come out on top.

Misstep #1: Zero Prep

With the ease of the internet, there's no reason Melissa and Dave should have shown up at the closest dealership to walk away with two SUVs and a whopping $88,050 in debt! It's never been easier to calmly and rationally decide on the type of vehicle that will match your needs and desires by doing a few hours of research over the span of a week or two in the comfort of your own home.

Misstep #2: Hungry Parents, Cranky Kids

Tired, hot, and hungry after a hectic week following a big move, Melissa and Dave fell victim to some bad decisions. I'm sure you've found yourself in a similar situation, but when avoidable, I'd advise not making any decisions that will cost you almost $100,000 in this state.

Did you know that judges are 65 percent more likely to grant parole after lunch?[14] Considering the fact that judges are highly educated, experienced, and supposedly impartial authority figures, you wouldn't think such a major decision could be so drastically swayed by a full stomach. But if judges can't think straight on an empty stomach, then you probably can't either. The study revealed that it wasn't just low blood sugar that affected a judge's decision, but rather a depletion of their cognitive capacity caused by decision fatigue.

On top of the hunger and exhaustion, Melissa and Dave were likely also suffering from decision fatigue. Think about all the decisions you make in a day: Did you get up right away this morning or hit the snooze button? Should you wear the green striped shirt or the white button-up? Did you have coffee at home or Starbucks on the way to work? Will you ask your colleague to go for lunch or eat at the deli on your own? I'm tired just thinking about it!

Each day you make dozens, if not hundreds, of microdecisions. If at the end of the day you have to make a major decision like buying a car, a house, or even a suit that you saw on sale, you might suffer from decision fatigue. You're more likely to buy something you don't need or want, fail to accurately calculate the costs, neglect to consider your options, or worse, fall prey to someone else's decision—whether that's a retailer, financial institution, or salesperson. I'd advise being very cautious, and if possible, take the day off work when you're making major life decisions or purchases. This advice can also be applied when choosing or meeting with your financial planner, getting a mortgage or life insurance, or setting up your child's RESP—to name a few.

Misstep #3: Reciprocity Rule

Melissa and Dave shouldn't have taken the cold water and pretzels from Michael. Sounds extreme? Let me explain.

If you do something for me today, you'll likely expect that I will return the favour later. That's reciprocity, and it's been necessary for survival throughout history. The funny thing about reciprocity is that it's so deeply rooted that we often unconsciously want to pay people back. Unfortunately, this means that we can very easily be exploited by retailers and salespeople.

Even the smallest gesture can establish a feeling that you "owe" the other person. Subconsciously, Melissa and Dave felt like they owed Michael their business in exchange for the water, pretzels, and his time. If you're planning on committing a few hours to buy a car, come prepared with your own water and snacks for you and your children. That way, you'll avoid the possibility of a salesperson giving you something that endears you to them, which might then necessitate returning the favour.

Misstep #4: Not Crunching the Numbers

Melissa and Dave didn't prepare for the extra costs that came attached to undercarriage protection, loan protection, disability protection, and other admin fees.

Retailers—especially car dealers—are experts at giving us small numbers that seem manageable. I'm sure you've heard something along the lines of "It's only a few dollars a day/week/month, and then you too can be happy and live a fulfilling life with this new _____." So tempting!

When you crunch the numbers and see the entire cost—over a year *and* the entire term of the financing (if paying with a credit card, getting a loan, etc.), the larger sum engages a different—more rational—part of your brain. But sometimes we don't think clearly, especially if the total cost is buried in a mountain of fees under less than ideal circumstances—such as getting your car loan or mortgage at the end of a busy day. Your brain is likely to gloss right over it! Does your brain mysteriously tune it out? It's not exactly a scientific answer, but I believe that's more or less what happens.

It's just too much for our brains to comprehend when we are focused on something else. You just want to get the car, get the financing process over with, and get the keys. It's easy to overlook something like a few tens of thousands of dollars in interest. So once you've had time to settle from the rush and stress of the process, pull those discarded documents out of their drawer. You might be able to pay the loan off sooner than you think.

Misstep #5: Influence

We're much more influenced by what's around us than we would like to admit—all the cool kids are doing it, so you want to too. When Dave and Melissa moved to Alberta, they noticed that they didn't fit in because they didn't have a truck or SUV like their neighbours. It's a common problem, and the urge to be the "norm" can start to creep into your subconscious. For Dave and Melissa, this urge cost them over $100,000. It's good to be conscious of how your surroundings can influence you and to know when (and when not) to give in.

The reason to make a purchase might be about more than just having the best new product, as was the case for Dave and Melissa. Their neighbours were all driving SUVs and trucks because of the terrible winter driving conditions in Alberta, so Melissa and Dave assumed an SUV or truck would be the only safe option. This is when research, once again, plays an important role. Get to know why everyone is doing something a certain way, and then decide if it is best for you.

And as an Alberta native who has driven Highway 2—the stretch between Calgary and Edmonton—countless times, I'll attest that there are always more SUVs and trucks in the ditches than any other vehicle. In part this is because there are more SUVs and trucks on the road in the first place, but I also believe that drivers of these bigger vehicles rely too heavily on the power and handling of their car, and don't focus on actually driving the roads safely and with control themselves. I'm not suggesting you shouldn't listen to your peers about what has worked for them, only that you educate yourself so that you can then decide if getting what your neighbour has is really the best option for you.

Misstep #6: Car Poor

Melissa and Dave resorted to draining their emergency fund to be able to afford two new SUVs. Now they are car poor *and* have to stress about replenishing their emergency fund.

Did you know that money stress can actually reduce your cognitive capacity, temporarily affect your IQ, and hinder your problem-solving skills, according to Dr. Moira Sommers, a neuropsychologist specializing in money issues?[15] So, just when you need your brain to help you figure a way out of your money woes, its ability is reduced, thus the need to reach out for help to a pro like a Certified Financial Planner or nonprofit credit counsellor.

Buying too much of anything—whether it's a car out of your price range, a new house, or any consumer product—can leave you stressed, which takes away from your ability to enjoy the item you purchased. When you're making a big buying decision, don't do it in one fell swoop. Distance yourself. Go for a coffee. Sleep on it. Talk to a friend. Better yet, figure out what you won't be able to have. With our car example, if you buy beyond your means and stretch your budget, not only will you likely suffer from sleepless nights, but you will also close the door on other opportunities that you'll no longer be able to afford, such as travel, dining out, new clothes, toys, and other costly experiences.

Misstep #7: Opportunity Cost

Whenever you make a purchase—especially a large one—you'll want to consider what else you could have done with that money. What would you have enjoyed as much or more? How could that money have been invested to increase long-term enjoyment?

With just the depreciation of both cars after driving off the lot, Melissa and Dave could have taken the entire family for a vacation, if not several. They likely thought they didn't have money for a vacation so soon after their big move, and yet they found enough money to buy two SUVs. By impulsively buying their vehicles without examining the opportunity costs, they missed out on other ways they could have spent that money and the pleasures associated with those opportunities. Perhaps Dave could have used the funds to start a side business that would turn a profit in two years, or Melissa could have invested in her education, which would have increased her salary by 20 percent in the next three years. Or, they could have both had lattes every day and taken the kids to Disneyland, twice. The opportunities are there, you just have to decide what's worth your money.

THE SOLUTION?

Unfortunately, Melissa and Dave depleted their emergency savings for a depreciating asset since all cars drop in value the day you drive them off the dealer's lot. They have two young kids and have just moved across the country, and the SUVs were not the best use of their emergency fund. They'll have to rebuild that safety net and reassess how they spend their funds to get the most out of their money for their family. You'll see that with a mixture of research, preparedness, and simply broadening the conversation about money and financial priorities with your family, you can make big purchases (like a car or two, for example) more wisely. In case you find yourself in the same or a comparable situation as Melissa and Dave, I'll walk you through how the process should go and show you where you can learn from their mistakes.

Step #1: Do Your Research

There is so much information available to us that you should never go into a shopping trip blind. Whether it's for a car, a printer, or even a new suit, there are countless reviews to peruse online, as well as forums and publishers dedicated to answering common questions about most consumer products. I know research can seem daunting—maybe the idea of research brings up memories of cold library stacks and endless work—but I promise, it's easier than that.

Get online, buy some magazines (*Consumer Reports* does a car issue every year), and get an idea of what vehicles cost, what brands are within your price range, and features that you are looking for. If you do your research right, you'll also get a sense of the different dealer incentives you might encounter, such as cash back, a lower interest rate on financing or leasing, or free oil changes for life. The research possibilities are endless, but generally my rule is I don't stop until I'm satisfied with the information I've gathered. Google, read articles, ask questions on Reddit or of your friends in real life (IRL)—gather everything you can about hidden fees, sales tactics, and what can and cannot be negotiated at a car dealership. If you run out of resources, pick up a consumer guide to help you choose the best makes and models based on what's important to you in a vehicle. Depending on how detailed you get with your research, this could take as little as just over an hour of your time, but it could save you big in the long run.

Step #2: Make a Five-Year Plan

Again, this doesn't only apply to car shopping. Sure, a five-year plan might sound a little vision boardy, but from a financial perspective, it's good to think about where you'll be in five years and what you'll need to get there. What are your big life goals for the next five years? To help get the ball rolling, here are some things I consider when planning out my finances ahead of time like this:

- Will you go on vacation? Are you planning any big trips that will substantially cut into your savings?
- Do you want to buy a house? If not, do you plan on making any costly renovations or upgrades to your current house or apartment? Do you have any upkeep costs to take into consideration?
- Do you need to start an emergency fund? If you already have one, do you need to keep contributing to it to help it grow to its full potential?
- Do you want to start an investment account?

Once you have a five-year plan in mind, you can budget accordingly and get a sense of what you can actually afford to spend now on a down payment and in the future on monthly payments.

Step #3: Crunch the Numbers

Once you know what you can afford, get online and browse the car dealership's websites to figure out what it's really going to cost to buy the make and model you're interested in, along with all the bells and whistles. Do you want a sunroof, automatic locks, or maybe an automatic starter (that always sounds tempting in the dead of winter)? With the cost in mind, you can determine where you can find the money to fund your new purchase.

Dave and Melissa unwisely exhausted their emergency account to pay for their SUVs, but that's never the best option. As you learned in the "Cash or Credit?" chapter, an emergency account should contain at least three to six months' worth of your household income and should be kept in a safe, available account in case of emergencies. Although Dave and Melissa's emergency account had enough in it to cover the down payments on their cars, they should have explored other options rather than deplete an account that would otherwise provide a financial and emotional buffer in the case of real emergencies.

Ideally, you should actually be able to afford your purchases when the time comes to make them, but if not, consider using a line of credit instead. As long as you're responsible with your debt, and you won't be tempted to use a line of credit for whatever your heart desires, then it's a great option. Generally, a secured line of credit can be obtained with low to no cost from your bank. Once it's set up, you will normally get a prime rate, especially if you're in good standing with the bank and have a great credit score. Finally, if you have a line of credit, it won't cost you anything until you have to use it. If you do have to use it—in this case, to make the down payments on a car—you could make interest-only payments until you get back on your feet and pay it off in full.

Step #4: Get a Financing Rate

Contact your banker to see what financing rate is available to you. With that information in hand, you'll be able to decide if you should receive financing directly from the car dealership, if you should look into leasing options, or if you'd be better off choosing a loan from your own bank. Consider contacting a Certified Financial Planner (such as a fee-only financial planner) as well to help you figure out the best options for you. You'll want to take all costs into consideration and verify that there aren't any blind spots you might have missed—for example, if you're in a high tax bracket, would it make sense to invest in an RRSP and take your tax refund to help with the car purchase?

> ### *Where Is My Money Going?*
>
> Generally, in the investment world, planners, advisors, and mutual fund salespeople receive a commission based on the money you invest with them (or the investments they buy on your behalf). They can also receive compensation for every year that you invest with them—this is a trailing fee and incentivizes the financial professional to provide you with exceptional, ongoing service.
>
> Certain professionals are what we call "fee-only" planners. They don't represent any particular product or service, and instead provide planning services (such as financial, tax, retirement, or estate advice) by charging you directly, either by the hour or by the plan. The associated fees vary person by person, so I suggest that you shop around and ask many questions. If you're looking for this type of service, you'll want to ensure the person is a Certified Financial Planner and in good standing with FP Canada, which regulates financial planners in Canada.

Professionals at the car dealerships want to get the most money out of you as possible. On the other hand, financial professionals want to ensure that you keep as much of your money in the bank or in investments as possible, so it really can be worthwhile to do the work of getting a professional opinion before a big shopping trip.

Step #5: Go Shopping

It's shopping day! Now that you're prepared, with your research in hand and your financial bandwidth in mind, you're ready for the big purchase. Set yourself up for success by removing any distractions. If possible, leave the kids at home with a babysitter. Have a good meal beforehand so that you're not hangry. Take the afternoon off and go during a quiet weekday if you can manage it. Bring your own water and fill your glovebox with snacks. And no matter what you do, do not buy from the dealer today! This is a big purchase. Take the time to process it all and to discuss your decision with those close to you whose opinion you value.

Step #6: Go for a Test Run

Rent a model as close to your vehicle of choice as possible. Use the rental car to drive your normal routine on both a day you have to work and a day you have off. You want to get a feel for the car as you would use it in your everyday life. Complete activities your family would normally do—put the kids in their car seats, throw the golf clubs and hockey bag in the trunk or back seat, get groceries, and drive into the city and around the neighbourhood a few times. Does the car meet your needs?

I imagine some of you are thinking, "You want me to spend money on a rental car? I thought you were going to teach me how to save money?" Hear me out. When you test-drive a car at the dealership, you don't get the real experience. The car dealer hovers over you like the worst back-seat driver, and you might get to go around a few blocks to make sure the brakes work and the acceleration isn't too abrupt, but you'll never get a sense of how the car will fit into your life in that short drive. So yes, I'm asking you to spend a little money on a car rental to save big in the long run. You don't want to buy a car you'll regret purchasing after driving it for a few days.

Step #7: Shop Right

When you're satisfied with your decision and ready to make the purchase, go to the dealership to buy the car. Do so near the end of the day, at the end of the week, and at the end of the month. Salespeople and dealerships are most likely to make a deal with you at these times because they need to reach or exceed their quotas. They're more hopeful at the start of their day and are, therefore, less likely to negotiate, but at the end of the day, they'll be fatigued and more willing to approve your demands for a deal or add-ons. Conversely, at the beginning of the month they have lots of time to reach their sales goals, so they'll still be feeling refreshed and optimistic about their prospects. Just make sure you're not fatigued! Go shopping feeling refreshed on a day where you haven't had to make too many decisions.

Finally, don't let the dealer persuade you to trade in your old car, unless you've already decided that's your best option. You should know going into the dealership how you plan to handle your trade-in—whether you want to sell it yourself online or negotiate the trade-in as part of your new purchase. As part of your earlier research, you should be able to determine the value of your current vehicle.

If all goes according to plan, you can be the happy owner of a new or leased car in just a few short steps. A car is arguably the second-largest purchase of your life, and by taking the time to make an informed decision, you could save yourself hundreds or thousands of dollars and years of buyer's remorse.

WHERE ARE THEY NOW?

Melissa and Dave quickly realized their mistake in buying two SUVs and made an appointment with a financial professional. While they couldn't afford her fees right away, they made an appointment for six months out and saved in advance to pay for the quote they'd been given for three hours of her time. After the meeting, they exhaled a huge sigh of relief. They have a long way to go to replenish their emergency funds, but they now have a plan.

They have a road map to pay their car payments down sooner and are on track to start saving for their retirement in the near future. Working through the numbers with their planner has helped them set clear goals, and they've established how they're going to get there. Their planner even set up a vacation fund, and they're excited to plan a trip with the twins for the near future. The best part is that all of this will be done with money that will be saved in advance—zero guilt!

To combat the cost of the cars, they cancelled the hidden disability and other insurance on both their loans because they already have exceptional coverage with their employers. This saved them $6,500 over the life of their loans.

Three years after they bought their SUVs, the dealership invited them to a swanky event: an evening of music, wine, and cheese. Now aware of the reciprocity rule, Melissa and Dave were hesitant to accept, but their kids were away at a friend's house that night and it seemed like a fun, free night out. At the event, the salesperson offered them a deal that seemed too good to be true: They could trade in one or both of their vehicles for a brand-new one at their current payment. They were not the only ones being offered this deal and could see others at the event were all smiles and excitement. Melissa and Dave gave each other a look, and a beat later they blurted out, "Can we have that in writing to think about?" They had learned their lesson!

With the offer in writing, they rang up their financial pro and found that the deal was in fact too good to be true. By keeping the same payment for a newer vehicle, they would be required to extend their loan out another three years—increasing their current loan to eight years. With only five years left on their current car payments, they both agreed to say "No!"

Today, they're enjoying their SUVs and finding ways to pay the loan down sooner, and they are excited that when the payments are done they can head back to their financial professional to figure out where the monthly payment can be redistributed.

Dave has started to work more from home, and they're considering selling one of the vehicles because they can rely on car sharing programs in Alberta when they need the use of a second car. Dave has calculated that they can save over $10,000 a year by eliminating the insurance, gas, and monthly car payments on one of their vehicles, and they can invest whatever profits they make selling the car.

They'll survive this car-nundrum, but they've certainly learned their lesson about making impulsive and costly financial decisions.

6

Sharing Is Caring

Whether you consolidate all your income, have one joint account, or keep all of your finances separate, sharing money with a partner can be a struggle. Simply talking about money with a partner can be uncomfortable, and since we don't often choose a life partner based on whether they share our views on money, when the discussion finally arises, it can get heated. If you haven't seriously thought about your own financial beliefs, it would not be surprising if these issues cause tension in your relationship. But it doesn't have to be this way!

Denise was single for most of her twenties and learned to be independent from a young age. However, when she met and then married Lucas, both her financial and romantic relationship status changed. Lucas was used to having control of his finances, so Denise let him take the reins. They merged their money into one account, she started to use the supplementary cards on his accounts rather than her own, and she lost track of her financial independence. Twenty-two years later, she found herself in the middle of a messy divorce and scrambling to gain back her money sense. Having to start from scratch, Denise was frustrated that she had given her partner total financial control.

It's now been a few years since her divorce, and she's regained financial order, but she's dating someone new, and things are starting to get serious. She and Ethan are even talking about moving in together, so this time Denise wants to make sure she and her partner are on the same page about how they'll handle their finances.

WHERE SHE WENT WRONG

Denise was confident about keeping track of her money when she had to be, but she gave up all financial responsibility at the request of her first husband. If they had had an open conversation about how much control Lucas would have over their finances, Denise might have been able to maintain some control over her financial know-how and standing. Denise also lost any interest in keeping up-to-date with her own personal financial education, which meant she had to start from scratch once she and Lucas split up.

Misstep #1: Abdicating Responsibility

As a young adult, Denise loved learning about personal finance and did her best to get a base knowledge of the more complex capital markets. When she and Lucas got married, he offered to manage their shared finances, and that was the end of the conversation. When they split up, Denise had to face the terrifying reality that she didn't know her own financial standing. Where would she start?

In hindsight, Denise remembers that Lucas used to ask for her input when making major decisions such as how to invest in their

RRSP and their TFSA. At one point, she had more financial knowledge than Lucas, but she lost both her interest and awareness over time. Denise assumed that he would do what was best for them, and she stopped contributing to the conversation about their finances. She willingly lost control of her money.

In Canada, women are far from achieving financial equity—both in terms of pay and money management, so Denise is not alone in this problem. According to a recent survey by FP Canada, nearly 40 percent of women say they know very little about finance and investments, while 28 percent of Canadian women are dependent on a partner or someone else to make ends meet financially. Not only are women relying on others for support, but the research shows that women are also lacking in experience and education: Nearly 40 percent aren't comfortable negotiating a better interest rate, over half of Canadian women don't have a written financial plan, and 42 percent don't know their credit score.[16] This lack of education, execution, and empowerment can cost women tens of thousands of dollars over their lifetime.

Misstep #2: Lack of Communication

Throughout their relationship, Denise and Lucas often argued about leftovers. She'd make extra food at dinner to ensure there'd be enough for lunch the next day, but Lucas hated having to eat the same meal a second time. They'd fight about it, but they never explored the origin of Lucas's resentment toward leftovers or Denise's insistence on making them. If they'd had an open conversation about the relationship they'd had to food and money as children, they'd both have had a better understanding of where these habits originated.

Lucas grew up in a lower-income family, and he and his siblings knew when budgets were tight. He was encouraged to get a job when he was a teen, and his parents regularly taught him to save money. As a consequence of having to eat leftovers as a child, Lucas vowed he'd never suffer through the same meal twice as an adult. Denise, on the other hand, was raised by her grandmother and had no sense of her family's income. Her grandmother, who had lived through the Depression, thought that talking about (or wasting) money was a sin. Denise was taught by her grandmother to make a little more at each meal because you never knew if there would be food the next day and to never waste food.

Unfortunately, talking about money is still taboo in many relationships, but the lack of communication can be toxic. If Denise and Lucas had known each other's triggers about leftovers, perhaps Denise would have happily made less to save Lucas from having to relive the scarcity of his childhood. Often, the mundane issues we bicker about stem from deeply rooted money issues. Talk it out!

Misstep #3: Financial Infidelity

Denise and Lucas certainly did their fair share of hiding purchases from each other when they felt like they were spending beyond their budget. Lucas kept his motorcycle in his friend's garage for years, knowing Denise would never see the payments on his credit card statements. Similarly, Denise would sneak in purchases from her car when Lucas was out of the house and would use cash to make the payments so that he remained unaware.

Financial infidelity is more common than you'd think and can tear even the most solid relationships apart over time. According to a recent FP Canada and Credit Canada survey, one in three Canadians has been a victim of financial infidelity. The survey also found that 34 percent of those in a relationship kept financial secrets from their romantic partner and 36 percent lied about a financial matter. Single adults between the ages of eighteen and fifty-four are the most common victims of financial unfaithful-ness.[17] You're just cheating yourself by not being honest about your personal finances. Honesty really is the best policy when it comes to money.

Misstep #4: Hiding Past Financial Burdens

Denise learned about Lucas's past financial hardships only when they first heard they were not approved to get a mortgage for their dream home, for which they'd already put in an offer. Lucas's credit score was terrible, and he had multiple accounts sitting in collec-tions. It was only at this point that Denise started to think about just how much debt Lucas had before they met.

It took three years to save for a larger down payment, and her resentment toward Lucas only grew during that time. With De-nise's nearly perfect credit, the bank finally granted their request for a mortgage, but they never recovered as a couple. They had lost trust in each other. Their relationship, and Lucas's credit score, might have been salvaged if they had been open with each other about the financial baggage they each brought into the relation-ship.

Misstep #5: Fighting over Shame

Denise and Lucas never clarified how they wanted to share money, so they never delineated who would pay for what and when. As a result, they developed resentment toward each other when they couldn't buy luxury items that they both wanted. When they made an impulse purchase, they would hide it from each other until it inevitably surfaced—at which point they'd spiral into a fight fueled by shame. It always felt like they were being scolded, just like they were teenagers.

They simply weren't on the same page about their finances. Now that Denise has been on her own for a while, she's started to pick up the pieces of her financial life, and can set her own spending rules. Whether you're single or in a relationship, you should always have a financial plan, and follow bite-sized, consistent steps to meet your goals.

THE SOLUTION?

When it comes to sharing money in families or partnerships, I have seen it all. There's no one right way to do it, but communication and education should always be key aspects of any relationship involving money.

Step #1: Learning Self-Efficacy

When you're facing a new or overwhelming task, you might have to relearn something called *self-efficacy*: believing that the actions you take are going to make a difference. Even if you are an exceedingly confident parent, soccer coach, litigator, construction worker, etc., there will be certain situations where you need more help.

In the wake of Denise's divorce, her confidence and self-efficacy were both incredibly low. She made a list of everything she needed to do to get up-to-date on her own financial life after Lucas handled it for so many years. By following bite-sized steps, Denise knew what she needed to do and when to meet her goals over a six-month period.

Denise's Six-Month, Bite-Sized Plan

Month One

- **Week One and Two:** Locate all of your monthly bills and statements. Check online for electronic copies if you can't track down the paper copies.
- **Week Three:** Create a storage solution for incoming bills. This could be a basket in your front hall or an email folder for electronic bills. Create a filing system for bills you have paid—a separate accordion file or another email folder.
- **Week Four:** Set up an emergency savings account. You can do this in person at your bank or online.

Month Two

- Start the Thirty-Day Anti-Budget (see chapter 4) to see where and how you are spending your money.
- Check your insurance policies. Do you have coverage? Do you need more? What coverage do you have at work? Is it the right policy for you or should you have a stand-alone policy? Do you have mortgage insurance? Do you have insurance on your credit cards, and is it right for you? Do you have disability insurance or critical illness insurance in the event of a major health crisis?

Month Three

- Dig into your employer benefits plan if you have one. What options exist? Do you have a group RRSP? Are you maximizing your benefits? How have you invested in your RRSPs?
- Shop around for a lawyer and accountant depending on your situation and level of involvement. If you can afford to hire external help, it's good to start researching early to ensure you find a good fit. But if you can't afford it, or you are confident in your ability to tackle the upcoming documents alone, then you can forego this step.

Month Four

- Review, complete, or update your will.
- Review or create your power of attorney and personal directives—how you wish to handle your health issues.
- Check to see who you've listed as your beneficiaries. Who have you listed on your pension at work, your group RRSP, individual RRSP, TFSA, and life insurance policy? Do they align with your will?

Month Five

- If you don't have one already, set up an RRSP and/or TFSA if it's right for you.
- If you already have investments, find out more about them. How is your money invested? Are they right for you? What fees are you paying?

- Create a financial plan that includes a strategy for current life goals, insurance, tax planning, retirement, and whatever else suits your lifestyle. If you already have a financial plan, now's the time to review it!
- Review your income. Can you increase it? Maybe you can ask for a raise or do freelance work on the side?

Month Six

- Automate your life as much as possible. What reoccurring bills can you pay automatically so you don't have to think about them? Is your employer taking enough in taxes out of your monthly pay so you don't owe more at the end of the year? Have you created automatic deposits for your emergency savings accounts and other investments such as an RRSP or TFSA?
- Review your work from the past six months, and give yourself a big pat on the back!

If you need to get your financial life in order, this list can help you too. Even if the tasks are different or more specific to your situation, it's helpful to spread them out over a six-month period so that it all feels manageable. With every item that you check off, you'll feel that much closer to turning your financial life around.

As Denise worked on regaining financial control of her life, she struggled with what author and psychologist Carol Dweck calls a "fixed" mindset, as opposed to a "growth" mindset. With a fixed mindset, Denise was holding herself back from taking action, and you may be facing a similar problem if you've ever had to face a tough task—whether it's physically or emotionally difficult—and then stopped partway through when it became too hard or you convinced yourself that it was not manageable. With a growth mindset, on the other hand, you acknowledge that you can in fact accomplish the task with the right help and information. Remind yourself that others have survived worse situations and that it's okay to not know everything. Give yourself permission to be on a journey, and embrace a growth mindset rather than a fixed mindset.

Step #2: Get Financially Healthy

If you were trying to improve your physical health, most experts would suggest you do three things: weigh in, keep track, and get help. It's not so different when you're trying to improve your financial health. Denise has to have a basic understanding of her finances before she can even think about sharing money again in a new relationship. These three steps can help her—and you—gain back some financial control and confidence. Here's how to weigh in, keep track, and get financial help:

- Weigh in. Start by determining how much money you have and how much money you owe. Here are some questions to help kick-start that process:
  - *What are your monthly payments?*
  - *What are the interest rates associated with your*

debts, and how much does that interest cost you each month?

- *What investments do you have? What are the fees associated with those investments?*
- *What benefits do you have at work?*
- *What are you missing in your financial life? Do you have mortgage insurance, life insurance, disability insurance, a will, powers of attorney, etc.?*

■ **Keep track.** Using the Thirty-Day Anti-Budget, you should be able to determine how much you are spending on a monthly basis. Make a conscious effort to track how much of your money is spent on "empty" purchases that could instead be put toward saving, paying down debt, or having more mindful fun, such as a vacation.

■ **Get help.** Just as you might hire a personal trainer to guide your physical health, you should consider hiring a professional to help guide you toward your financial goals. With the help of a financial professional, nonprofit credit counsellor, banker, lawyer, and/or Chartered Professional Accountant, you'll have the guidance you need to get control of your finances.

Step #3: Set Yourself Up for Success

A big part of financial success is good organizational skills. You already know I'm not going to suggest you create a budget, but there are ways to arrange your life to better organize your funds. After allowing Lucas to run her finances for so long, Denise has to organize her way to success!

Start with a basket. Getting your financial life in order starts by gathering your paperwork together. Leave a basket or another container on top of your fridge or in your front hall—wherever you open your bills as they come in. When you open a bill, you can put it in the basket once you've set a reminder in your calendar or phone app to pay it. If you have enough money coming in each month to pay all of your bills, set up automatic payments. However, it's still best to review all of your bills every month to verify that there are no fraudulent purchases on your account and that you haven't been overcharged for anything.

A Note on Going Digital

If you, like many people, receive your bills and statements electronically, take the time to review them for accuracy and as a reminder of the money going out of your accounts. With digital bills, it's too easy for your money to be out of sight, out of mind, and you don't want that to derail your tracking and monitoring of your financial life.

Create a filing system. I use an accordion file, which only set me back around $20, and it's well worth the money. It holds all of my important documents like my bank and credit card statements, tax notices, mortgage documents, insurance, and more. Whatever filing system you use, I find it's helpful to sort my documents by year. At the end of every month, empty your basket of bills (ensuring they've been paid) and file them away. Shred, don't toss, any documents with your name or any account information that you don't need or that aren't required to back up your tax filings.

Lock some things away. Lock up your most sensitive documents, such as your passport, SIN card, and birth certificate. It's good practice to take stock of these documents every quarter to ensure you know they'll be there when you need them.

When you're not travelling, keep your family's passports locked up. Documents that contain highly sensitive information (such as applications for your child's RESP, your RRSP, TFSA, RRIF, or mortgage and loan documents) can be used to steal your identity if they are found by the wrong hands. Lock them up!

A Note on Fraud

Financial fraud is on the rise, so it's important to be vigilant about checking your bank and credit card statements every month. Look for even the smallest purchases that you don't recognize. Often, fraudsters will test an account by charging a card with something that costs less than ten dollars. If they get away with the smaller purchase, they'll go for a big-ticket item. Depending on the terms and agreements associated with your bank and credit card company, you may only have thirty or sixty days to report a fraudulent charge, so checking your statements regularly will protect you from having to pay for these charges.

Build a money binder, for yourself and loved ones. Once you've found all of your statements, bills, professional contact information, and other important documents, make a list of them in the binder—it should be a snapshot of your financial life. It shouldn't contain the actual documents—those are filed away or locked up—but it should be a resource for you and your loved ones that includes important life details. You can type or write out the following:

- Associated account numbers for your:
  - *Bank accounts*
  - *Investment accounts*
  - *Pension or employee plans*
- The name and contact information for your:
  - *Financial Advisor or Certified Financial Planner*
  - *Lawyer*

- *Accountant*
- *Power of attorney*
- *Emergency contact(s)*

■ The location of your safety deposit box, if you have one

■ The name of the lawyer who handles your will

■ Details regarding your personal directives for health issues, if you have them

■ A list of bills/statements that you receive digitally

■ Any documents you haven't yet completed or are in the process of starting

Do not include your PIN or any passwords in this binder; simply listing the account numbers is enough for a loved one to locate and access your financial assets and debts. You should never write these passwords down or share them with anyone—it can open you up to fraud and nullify your fraud protection with your bank or credit card company.

Step #4: Create Your Net Worth Statement

Continuing with our theme of organizing your way to financial success, Denise needs to create her net worth statement to get a complete snapshot of her financial life. A net worth statement reveals how much you own and how much you owe to give you a full picture of your financial health. The exercise of calculating your net worth encourages you to dig through your assets and debts. As a result, you'll have a better idea of where you stand and what needs improving or refining. It'll be easy to determine once you've gathered all of your debts (what you owe) and assets (what you own). You can create a net worth statement individually or with a partner. Is it positive? Is it negative?

If it's negative, don't fret. It's normal to have a negative net

worth statement, especially if you own a house, if you've just grad-
uated from school and have significant student loan debts, and/or
if you are a new business owner. If your net worth statement causes
concern, the good news is that you now know where you stand.
From here, you can build a plan to move from a negative net worth
to a positive one. Don't forget, you can always reach out to professionals for help to get you there.

Step #5: Joint Accounts?

Denise and Lucas were constantly fighting about spending because
they shared all of their money. As a result, they often hid their purchases from each other, but it doesn't have to be that way!

If you have a partner, it's not always a simple task to merge and
share funds. There are several things to consider when making the
decision to have a joint account with a loved one. Imagine you have
a spotless credit record, no debt, and a nice nest egg for your future. Now, a partner enters the relationship with maxed-out credit
debt, no assets, and a poor credit score. If you were to merge all of
your funds into one account, you'd be taking on your partner's debt
and possibly damaging your otherwise clean record. So, it's important to consider your collective financial history when thinking
about creating a joint account or making any other decisions about
how you will share money in a relationship.

You have options. Some couples keep everything separate and
only split their day-to-day expenses. If you do create a joint account for the majority of your shared costs, it's a good idea for both
partners to have a separate account where a portion of the monthly
household income is deposited for individual, guilt-free spending.
Just because you're a couple doesn't mean you necessarily have to
account for absolutely every dollar you spend.

Step #6: Have the Talk

This isn't first-date material, but don't forget to have a conversation with your partner about money. Denise doesn't want to fall into the same financial trap with Ethan as she did with her ex-husband, but since talking about money is so hard for many people, she'll likely have to initiate the conversation and share her own financial baggage before encouraging Ethan to share his money challenges. If you want to get on the same page about money with your partner, here are some questions that can help:

- What are your financial goals?
- How much money do you make?
- How will you split your money for bills and spending?
- What kind of financial injuries and issues have you dealt with in the past? Do you still carry any financial issues or concerns?

Decades ago, employment contracts suggested that you should keep your salary confidential—not just from coworkers, but also from your spouse! And we haven't adapted much since then. A recent survey revealed that 43 percent of couples in the US didn't know their partner's salary, because talking about money is still taboo.[18] But, if you can move past the awkwardness of it, a serious discussion with your partner about money will go a long way in creating an open and healthy relationship.

Step #7: Ask the Hard Questions

Denise is nervous about having the money talk with Ethan because she doesn't want him to think she's interrogating him. But if you approach the conversation with cautious curiosity with the aim to learn more about your partner, you might be surprised at people's willingness to share.

If you've never talked about money with your partner, don't expect to have all the answers after just one conversation. It's a process, so make it as fun as you want (or can)! For many couples, it can take three to six sessions to get through it all. Here are six questions to get you and your partner on the same page about money:

1. What does money mean to you?

This is a great way to start the conversation, and it's normal to have more than one answer. Verbalize or write down as many as you can. Is there one word that best describes how you feel about money? What about your partner? What does that mean to you both?

If *freedom* is your answer, what does having financial freedom mean to you? Does it represent the ability to spend whenever you want, without constraints? A desire for financial freedom might also reveal a tendency to spend beyond your means. If your partner's answer is *security*, they might strive to save for the future, but are likely frugal and adverse to risk.

Knowing what money means to you and your partner can reveal a lot about your spending and saving patterns. If your opinions about money differ, you may be prone to disagreements, but it could also be good for your relationship—you can help balance each other out. If you're a spender, you can loosen up your frugal partner. If you're a saver, you can curtail your spend-happy partner.

2. How do you feel about money?

This question is subtly different, but important. If you don't know how you feel about something that controls so much of our daily life, you won't be able to take steps to improve your financial life. Does money make you feel stress, confusion, shame, discomfort, power, or unease? There's no right or wrong answer, as long as you have some kind of answer.

3. What are your earliest money memories?

Knowing what you and your partner picked up from childhood and family dynamics will give you both a glimpse into your relationship with money today. Did you talk about money in your family growing up? Did money run out quickly in your family? Did anyone ever take money from you or your family? Were you aware of your family's financial status?

Reserve judgment on yourself and your partner as you work through this question—this is not an exercise in blame, guilt, or shame. Hopefully, gaining an awareness of your past experiences with money will help reveal and shine a light on your current financial situation.

For questions four and five, you and your partner should write down your answers separately before sharing them with each other. This way, neither of you will be tempted to copy the other.

4. What are my goals? What are our goals?

What major accomplishments do you want to achieve? Do you want to go back to school, take a sabbatical, or buy a house? What major accomplishments does your partner hope to achieve? Compare notes. Are there major difference between your lists? Does one of you want something that conflicts with the other? It's best to know from the beginning if you'll need to make compromises in your relationship or if you'll both be able to realize your goals.

5. What do you need? What do you want?

The answers to these questions should reflect short-term desires, such as furnishing your home office, renovating the basement, or taking a holiday. Once you've both made your separate lists, come together to compare notes and make a master list of all your needs and wants. What are your top picks that you can tackle together? Are there any items on the list that will have to wait?

6. How are we going to get there?

Based on your previously calculated net worth statement, what do you individually need to do to meet your big and small goals? Do you need to eliminate debt, make saving a priority, rent out your basement for more income, negotiate a higher salary, or move closer to work and sell your second car? These questions, and more, will come up as you and your partner work through your relationship to money.

Step #8: Develop an Action Plan

Now that you've completed the six questions together, you need a plan—and you don't have to do this alone. If you can afford it, hire a professional to help you see your financial blind spots and set you on the right path. If you're swimming in debt, you may wish to enlist the assistance of a nonprofit credit counsellor. A financial pro can help you figure out how to save, look at your spending, and create a plan to achieve your goals—both big and small. If this list of questions raises bigger issues between you and your partner, you may wish to seek out a therapist who specializes in money issues.

Step #9: Check Your Credit Report

Credit controls many parts of your life individually and as a couple. If you're in a relationship, both of your scores will matter as you go through life together. If Denise would have checked her credit while she was married to Lucas, she would have had a better awareness of their debt because, as you may remember, your credit report lists all of your current debt obligations, outstanding balances, and payments. Checking your credit report can be an easy indicator of whether or not you need to make improvements to increase your score. As a couple, have a look at your scores, but reserve judgement of yourself and your partner. It's not a life score—just a snapshot of how you've managed your debt and payments during a certain period of time. Once you know your score, you can work diligently to maintain it or improve it.

Step #10: Learn Together

As Denise and Ethan work to start their relationship with each other and with their money, they can both benefit from expanding their money knowledge together. If you're looking to improve your financial skills and learn even more about managing your finances, consider taking a course with your partner. Many nonprofit credit-counselling agencies have free classes throughout the year, or you can subscribe to a money magazine and read the personal finance section of your favourite magazine or newspaper.

WHERE ARE THEY NOW?

Denise has been steadily rebuilding her credit score by spending money on a credit card under her own name—she feels so good knowing that it's hers and that she's taking control of her finances. Every time Denise buys something with her card, she transfers the money online from her savings account to her credit card immediately. She's also set up some new routines to ensure she is focused on her financial well-being.

Every morning, Denise checks her bank account online while enjoying her first cup of coffee. Seeing her savings (and watching them grow) makes her feel more financially confident, and it acts as another reminder to pay off her previous day's credit card purchases. Every Friday, Denise checks her other investment accounts where she's set up an RRSP with a $150 monthly contribution as well as a TFSA with a $250 monthly contribution. While it can be difficult to create a new financial habit or behaviour, Denise read an article that suggested that it can be easier to make a new habit stick if you anchor it to a keystone habit—something you do every day such as drinking coffee or brushing your teeth. She's found that she now looks forward to her morning ritual of coffee and financial statements. This small step takes an extra five minutes during her morning routine, and she then rewards herself with fifteen minutes of reading the news online and perusing her social media before getting ready for work.

On Fridays, Denise wakes up fifteen minutes early to simply sort and review what she's spent each week. This habit was a little more difficult to follow consistently, so she's set a weekly reminder on her phone to alert her.

After Denise and Ethan went through the six hard questions— it took them two months to cover them all—they established a habit they both enjoy: sharing their money interactions with each other over wine on the weekend. Looking to expand their financial knowledge together, they took an investment course recently, where they met another couple who was similarly trying to get a handle on their finances. Now they meet monthly to try to expand their conversations about investments and money as they work on building their prosperity as a team.

7

Burn Your Mortgage

There was a seemingly mythical time, long ago, when mortgage interest rates were in the double digits and mortgage-burning parties existed. Homeowners with a mortgage vowed to get rid of the debt as quickly as possible and looked forward to the day when they'd throw a party to celebrate the burning of their mortgage. Today, with interest rates at an all-time low, we've been preemptively partying with our debt in tow and have simply forgotten to set a date for when we can be free of our mortgage.

For Scott and Allyson, a mortgage-burning party is the furthest thing from their mind. While they are busy enjoying life, something sinister is brewing under the surface—debt! They don't see it or feel it because they've been paying their mortgage and bills every month, and they still manage to save a modest 5 percent of their income. So, what's the problem? Well, they have a monster mortgage on their fancy house and have very little equity because they use what they built up with the line of credit attached to their home.

What is Equity?

As you pay down your mortgage, or if your house goes up in value, you build wealth called equity. You can tap into that wealth without selling or remortgaging your house by relying on a home equity line of credit (HELOC). As you make room on your mortgage (by paying it down, for example), you can borrow more and more from your HELOC, almost like using a credit card, and you pay interest only on what you use. The bank is protected by securing your HELOC against the built-up wealth in your house (equity), so the interest rate is vastly lower than a credit card—as low as 3.95 percent currently.

The family has never saved up for trips, entertainment, or any of the other costs associated with their very busy family of four. Their younger son, Brad, is sixteen and plays competitively in junior hockey, and Chad, eighteen, is a jujitsu champion. Both sports take the boys all over the country, and Chad even has to travel internationally for some of the tournaments. The costs for these extracurriculars really add up, but Scott and Allyson don't know how to say no. Their parents didn't have the money to put them in sports growing up, so they both vowed they would fully support their kids' dreams—but it's slowly taking a toll on their wallets.

At this rate, their mortgage is going to weigh them down until they are seventy-five years old. Although they are saving 5 percent of each paycheque for retirement, they are still growing their debt year after year because they are spending 140 percent of their income—yes, they always make a point to save each month, but they spend the rest of what they make and keep using their line of credit. Really, they're not saving at all. The debt they take on each year far exceeds their savings. Scott and Allyson are living in the moment— something many of us aspire to do—but they have some work to do to ensure they'll have enough money to live on in the future.

> ### *Break It Down*
>
> Here's the cost of Scott and Allyson's mortgage:
>
> Amount they currently owe on their mortgage and line of credit: $680,000
> Cost of buying their house five years ago: $580,000
> Approximate value of their home now: $887,000
> Years left to pay off their mortgage: 25
>
>   As Scott and Allyson worked to pay down their house, it gradually increased in value. Last year, they had more than 20 percent home equity, so they decided to refinance their mortgage to a new twenty-five-year amortization. As a result, they'll have lower monthly costs, but they'll be paying off their mortgage for a lot longer than when they first signed. They owe more now than when they bought their house because they keep treating their HELOC like an ATM.

WHERE THEY WENT WRONG

A mortgage isn't meant to be a life sentence. The process of getting a mortgage, becoming a homeowner, and working to pay it off is quite overwhelming, but you'll hopefully only have to go through it a few times in your life. So it's important to do it right. Once that mortgage document is signed, you might be tempted to file it away and never look at it again until renewal time (if you locked in a rate), but read it through thoroughly and make a plan to pay it off—one that you can actually stick to.

Let's dissect where Scott and Allyson went wrong, and what you can learn from their mistakes. You'll see that if you make your financial life a part of your routine and not an event to get through, you too can find financial success. Just as you can't eat a salad once and expect great health as a result, you can't simply get a mortgage and expect financial freedom to just follow.

Misstep #1: Lured and Lulled

Interest rates are still at historical lows, so Scott and Allyson don't feel compelled to pay down their debt. They only look at what they're required to pay on their mortgage and don't consider that they could be paying more. They signed their mortgage and threw the document in a drawer, only reviewing it last year to see their refinancing options. Even if your bank isn't asking for more money, it doesn't mean you can't pay ahead and get rid of your debt sooner—most mortgages allow you to pay extra every month or every anniversary year. Doing so could save you tens or even hundreds of thousands of dollars over the life of your mortgage. To their detriment, Allyson and Scott aren't currently focused on debt repayment, but are instead giving in to their every want and whim. They're also relying too heavily on their line of credit, which they keep maxing out, and they only pay the interest. Simply put, they'll never be free of that debt.

Allyson and Scott should be looking to get rid of their mortgage rather than using their equity to pay for a lifestyle they truly can't afford. If housing prices in their area drop one day, they'll no longer have that equity to rely on. At the rate they're spending, they'll never get to retire, but will have to keep working to cover their housing bills. The Financial Consumer Agency of Canada, our federal consumer watchdog, issued a warning a few years ago about people dipping into their home equity because it's become so common. Since 2011, the number of households taking out a HELOC has increased by a whopping 40 percent, and the average HELOC owner owes $70,000.[19] The lesson here is don't treat the wealth in your house as found money to withdraw as you would from an ATM.

The Basics

What is a mortgage? How is it different from a line of credit? What else should you know before buying a house?

A traditional mortgage

A long-term loan against your house, provided by a bank or lender. It requires you to make payments over a long period, over ten to twenty-five years (and sometimes more). Payments contribute to the principal and the interest. The majority of your initial payments will go toward interest.

Amortization

This is how long you have to pay off your mortgage. Think of it as the time it takes to pay a big debt. In Canada, you can have an amortization of up to twenty-five years. The government recently reduced it from thirty-five years because they didn't want people owning homes unless they could really afford it. The longer the amortization, the lower the payment. If you have a twenty-five-year amortization, your payments would be much lower than if you had had a fifteen-year amortization because you have ten more years to pay.

Fixed-Rate Term

The period for which you're locked into an interest rate with your bank. It would be very risky for both you and your bank to agree to a set interest rate for your full twenty-five-year amortization. A five-year fixed term is common, which means you'll have a set interest rate for the first five years of paying off your mortgage. If rates go up, you'll be happy because you're locked in to the lower one, but if rates go down, you'll still have to pay a higher rate than what's available—it's mutually beneficial. This rate agreement also locks you into that bank. If you want to switch banks, get a new rate, or pay off your mortgage before your term expires, you'd have to pay a penalty. Term options can range anywhere from six months to ten years.

Variable Term

As with a fixed-rate term, you are still locked in with your bank for the duration of a variable term, but your rate floats according to the prime lending rate. Briefly, the prime lending rate is the best possible rate you can get from your bank. It's based on your creditworthiness and is applicable to secured debt. Over the long-term, a variable rate mortgage will beat a fixed rate. However, if you're uncomfortable with a floating rate or think rates will increase, a fixed rate may be better for you and help you sleep at night knowing your payment and interest costs are fixed for the length of your term.

Lump sum payments

Most mortgages allow you to contribute a single, larger amount of money to pay off your principal rather than paying in smaller installments. Alternatively, you can increase your monthly payment amount.

Miss a payment and other flexibilities

This handy feature within many mortgages allows you to miss one full payment per year. This can be a much-needed financial respite in the case of an emergency or if you're facing a tight cash flow month.

Frequency of payment

You can choose to pay most mortgages monthly or on an acceler-ated bimonthly or weekly schedule.

A secured line of credit (also often referred to as a home equity line of credit [HELOC])

A line of credit is a lot like a credit card. You only pay interest if you use the "available credit." You can spend within your available credit, in which case you will owe a balance. You can just pay the monthly requested amount or pay it off entirely, any time, without penalty. But unlike a credit card, a line of credit comes with a much lower interest rate. Your line of credit gets implicated with your mortgage when you secure that line of credit against your house—meaning that if you fail to pay, the bank can seize your house as payment. This might sound scary, but securing your line of credit against your home will give you an even lower interest rate. The less risk the bank has if you miss a payment, the better your rate—but there are, of course, risks for the debtor. Keep in mind that the big banks in Canada won't foreclose on your home after one or two missed payments. In fact, more often than not, they'll give you a chance to work with them to get your mortgage caught back up. However, if your mortgage (or second mortgage) is with a small private lender, they could take legal action faster than a big bank.

Misstep #2: Making Interest-Only Payments

A mortgage has two parts: the principal (the amount you borrowed) and the interest. With a traditional mortgage, you have to make both principal and interest payments. If your amortization was twenty-five years and rates remained consistent, you'd be mortgage free in twenty-five years. Sounds good, right?

The problem is that it's becoming increasingly common for banks to offer a secured line of credit attached to your house when you apply for a mortgage: a readvanceable mortgage. The available limit of this line of credit can grow as you make payments to your mortgage principle. For example, if Allyson and Scott got a $300,000 mortgage and the bank initially gave them a $50,000 line of credit, as they pay down their mortgage, the available room on their line of credit will increase to $60,000 over ten years of payments. Imagine having a credit card limit that keeps going up without having to apply for it or agree to the increase.

If you're the kind of person who isn't regularly tempted and is super disciplined with their debt, this isn't a problem. Having that line of credit available can be great for when you need it—for an emergency, home renovation, or any other unforeseeable costs. For Scott and Allyson, the problem is they have maxed out their spending, and they don't know how to distinguish between a financial *want* and a *need*. They are not alone in this problem, but because a line of credit only requires you to pay the interest on it, you could theoretically never pay it off.

Misstep #3: Retiring with a Mortgage

Half of Canadians expect to go into their retirement with a mortgage.[20] The habit of dipping into your house's equity is becoming increasingly common, so this number is unfortunately likely to increase. Set a goal of entering retirement with zero debt, which should include a paid-off house. Allyson and Scott are taking advantage of the fact that interest rates are still at historical lows in the wrong way. They are merely increasing their debt because it's "cheap" to service (paying the interest-only payments), but this is a missed opportunity to become mortgage free sooner because it costs less to have that debt when compared to periods of high interest rates.

We used to say, "I can't afford it." Now, we say yes anyway but pay a price over a longer period as our debt increases with no end in sight.

Misstep #4: Out of Sight, Out of Mind

Scott and Allyson went through the highs and lows of getting approved for their mortgage, but as soon as it was signed, they filed the paperwork away, never to be looked at again. Little did they realize that they were not at the end of the mortgage process at all.

They are not alone in thinking the mortgage process can be that simple. As the host of the show *Burn My Mortgage*, I witnessed countless participants flinch at hearing the interest costs they'd owe over the life of their mortgage. The families were often embarrassed to face the reality and would request that I lower my voice so as to not let their neighbours hear about their financial shame. After a few episodes, the TV crew started grumbling about how the big, bad banks were going to profit from all that interest and were trying to keep us in the dark about the truth of our finances. But nothing could be further from the truth.

The banks are not hiding anything. Scott and Allyson would have known exactly how much they were paying in interest if they reviewed their mortgage documents—as would the participants on *Burn My Mortgage*. When you sign the paperwork for a mortgage, you have to initial beside the dollar amount of total interest and principal to acknowledge you realize what you're getting into. You can also visit your bank's website to use a mortgage calculator, which will help you determine the impact of bumping up your monthly or annual payment on your principal. You'd be surprised at how quickly you can become mortgage free.

The entire home-buying process is certainly overwhelming, and most of us will only do it once or a few times in our lifetime, so I understand if you just want it to be over. It can also be hard to process such a large amount of money, but as tempting as it might be to erase the memory and ignore the details of your mortgage, that will be to your own financial detriment.

Misstep #5: Keeping a Balance on High-Interest-Rate Credit Cards

Scott and Allyson had never maxed out their credit cards, but they also never paid the full amount due. As a result, they were paying 20 percent interest on their bank credit card and 29 percent interest on their department store credit cards. For them, it's adding up to a total of $2,400 a year. This money goes directly to the credit card companies when Scott and Allyson could instead be using that money to pay down their mortgage.

THE SOLUTION?

Feeling good about money requires that you pay regular attention to your financial well-being. It would be silly to think that going to the gym once or eating healthy periodically would create physical fitness. Becoming financially fit should be a lifelong process, not a hurdle to surpass and then never look back.

And the process doesn't have to be painful. You can't expect to make amends for slacking all week by running or working out like a fiend on Saturday and Sunday without suffering on Monday morning once the lactic acid in your muscles has built up. You'd be better off taking a brisk walk for ten or twenty minutes every day—and the same goes for your financial health. The key is consistency and working with bite-sized chunks that you can fit into your life.

Step #1: What Can You Afford?

The first question is simple: What can you afford? You should arm yourself with this knowledge before visiting the bank by referencing an affordability calculator found on most bank websites. At the bank, your lender will use the following calculations to determine what you can afford:

GROSS DEBT SERVICE (GDS) RATIO:

$$\frac{\text{Mortgage Principal} + \text{Mortgage Interest} + \text{Property Taxes} + \text{Heat} + \text{Condo Fees (if applicable)}}{\text{Gross Annual Income}}$$

Your total monthly housing costs (seen on the first line of the above formula) shouldn't be more than 32 percent of your gross annual income.

Gross or Net?

Gross income refers to total income before the deduction of any fees. Most commonly, gross income refers to income before tax deductions. Net income refers to total income after taxes are deducted. It's what you have left in your bank before paying any expenses.

TOTAL DEBT SERVICE RATIO (TDSR):

$$\frac{\text{Mortgage Principal + Mortgage Interest + Property Taxes + Heat +}}{\text{Condo Fees (if applicable)+ Other Debt Obligations}}$$
$$\overline{\text{Gross Annual Income}}$$

Your total debt cost shouldn't be more than 40 percent of your gross income. This includes your total monthly housing costs (as seen on page 137 in the GDS formula) plus any other debts, such as credit card payments, car payments, a line of credit, student loan debt, or child or spousal support payments.

Step #2: Check Your Credit Score

Using the skills you learned in the "Cash or Credit?" chapter, verify your credit score to determine if you have a good enough score to be approved for a mortgage. As you now know, your credit score is a snapshot of how you've paid your debts and how much outstanding debt you have. It gives the lender an idea of how likely you are to pay the debt they're considering granting you. Remember, banks and lenders are in the business of making money, so the better your score, the better your chance that not only will you be approved but that you can negotiate a better interest rate. Note though that your score isn't the only factor a lender looks at. They also consider your income and total debt owed.

Step #3: Do Some Research

Once you know what you can afford and your credit rating, the next step should be part of your process for any financial decision: research. Try out a few mortgage calculators online and get a sense of what to expect before you head off to the bank. Here are some questions you should be able to answer:

- How much of a down payment do you have or will you have saved?
- What amortization makes sense for you?
- Will you be paying monthly, biweekly, or weekly?
- Which payment schedule is best for your cash flow?

Step #4: Shop Around for a Rate

Back in the pre-internet dark ages, finding out what a bank charged for mortgage rates was difficult and time consuming. Luckily for you, it's much simpler today and just requires a quick search online. Every bank and lender posts their special rates online, but keep in mind that you can negotiate your loan, line of credit, and mortgage rate. It's as simple as asking about their best rate—this will often get the bank to bump down their advertised rate. If you're a good customer (if you've been with the bank for some time, have other services with them, aren't a credit risk, etc.), you can push the lender further for a better rate.

Mortgage Broker?

You may wish to use a mortgage broker to walk you through the approval and negotiating process. The benefit of using a broker is that they'll shop around to a number of lenders on your behalf to get you the best deal and rate. They don't charge you for their services, but they receive a commission from the lender. They also only pull your credit report once, so you don't have a bunch of banks setting off red flags on your credit report as would be the case if you were shopping around on your own. Brokers can also be great educators and partners in the mortgage approval process and can guide you on how to improve your situation if your mortgage is declined. Unfortunately, not all banks offer their services through a mortgage broker.

Step #5: Get Preapproved

Once you have an idea of your rate and the bank you're going to go with, you'll want to get preapproved. You can do this online, make an in-person appointment, or call up your bank to walk you through the process. The importance of getting preapproved is that it lets you know your budget before you go shopping or make an offer on a house. Getting preapproved doesn't require you to take the mortgage or buy a property, but it will give you the assurance that you'll get the mortgage for the amount the bank has approved you for when you are ready to buy.

Your preapproval will tell you the maximum amount of a mortgage you can afford and will provide you with an estimate of your payments as well as lock the interest rate for 60 to 120 days, depending on the lender or mortgage broker. To get preapproved for a mortgage, your lender will look at several financial factors, including:

- The size of your down payment.
- The total cost and type of house you're considering. Is it a cottage? Does the house need renovations before you can move in? Does it have a basement or garage suite that you can rent out? Will you have a renter to help offset the cost?
- Your gross income (before taxes). They will look at your net income if you're self-employed.
- Your expenses, including new estimated living costs and all utilities.
- All your debt.
- Your credit score.
- The interest rate. Will you be choosing a fixed or variable rate?
- The amortization period.

■ Your net worth.

Net Worth

To calculate your **net worth**, make a list of everything you own (your assets). This should include the investments you may have in or outside of a Registered Retirement Savings Plan (RRSP) or TFSA, property, a business interest, cash value life insurance, etc. Then, make a list of all your debts.

Total assets - total debts = net worth

Don't be worried if your net worth is negative if you are young or if you are a first-time home buyer. It doesn't mean you won't get approved for a loan or mortgage. As discussed above, approval is also based on income, credit score, and other determining factors.

Step #6: Get a Rate Hold

Once you are preapproved, you'll get a rate hold—this is the amount of time your bank or lender will guarantee your preapproved rate. Here are a few questions to ask your bank or lender pertaining to your rate hold:

■ How long will they guarantee the preapproved rate?
■ Will you automatically get the lowest rate if interest rates go down while you're preapproved?
■ Can the preapproval be extended?

Step #7: Go Shopping

Now that you've done your research, it's time to go and find your new home! Just because you were preapproved for a certain amount doesn't mean you have to run out and stretch your wallet to its limit. You might even be surprised by how much your bank or lender has approved for you to spend—it'll likely be much more than you thought. It's understandable if you're uncomfortable with the amount, and you may wish to hire a fee-only Certified Financial Planner to help you see your home-buying decision in the larger scope of your overall financial plan. You can always opt to spend less than you've been approved for.

Remember, you don't want to be house poor, which happens when you overextend your finances to buy a house that is out of your price range. You may still need to furnish your home, save for retirement, pay off other debts, and continue to live, of course! Even though interest rates are at an all-time low, if rates do go up, how will that affect you? Finally, keep in mind that lenders are in the business of making money. Just because you're being offered a certain preapproved amount doesn't mean that it's right for you and your unique situation.

Step #8: The Details

Now's the time to really dig into your mortgage contract. How much money do you want to borrow and how much can you afford to put toward your down payment? If you contribute less than 20 percent of the total amount as a down payment, you'll have to pay an insurance premium that protects the lender (in case you default). The insurance premium will depend on how much below 20 percent you contribute, if you're self-employed, and more.

You'll have to negotiate with your lender about a few key elements of your mortgage contract, including:

■ The amortization period: Remember, the longer it is, the longer you'll be paying, but the lower your payment will be.
■ The term: Are you going with a fixed or variable rate?
■ Frequency of payments.
■ And whether your mortgage will be open or closed.

Make sure to ask questions about your options within your mortgage contract, such as:

■ What happens if you want to pay it off sooner?
■ Can you increase your monthly payments? By how much?
■ Can you make lump sum principal payments? When and how much?
■ Are there options built into your contract that will protect you in times of financial trouble, such as a skip-a-payment option?
■ Can you change the frequency of your payments?
   • *Will you be paying weekly, biweekly, or monthly? Paying monthly will cost you the most over time. But, if you get paid monthly, that may make the most sense for the money flowing in and out of your life.*
   • *If you eventually want to change to making weekly or biweekly payments, can you do that and how?*
■ Are your property taxes included in your mortgage payment? If not, you'll want to set up a payment plan with your local municipality's tax department, as coming up with an annual lump sum can be tough for most home owners.
■ Is your down payment less than 20 percent? If so, your

lender will require that you pay for Canada Mortgage and Housing Corporation (CMHC) default insurance, which protects them in case you stop making your payments. It's only required on down payments under 20 percent because if you don't have that much invested in your house, it's easier for you to walk away if housing prices drop. The more equity or wealth you have in your house, the less likely you'll cease paying your mortgage.

- What are the closing costs, such as legal fees, land transfer taxes, and Realtor commissions? Will these be included in your mortgage, or will you have to pay them separately?

Mortgage 101

This is what your mortgage payments would look like on a $500,000 house with a few variables to consider:[21]

Mortgage Payments for an Asking Price of $500,000

Down Payment	5%	10%	15%	20%
	$25,000	$50,000	$75,000	$100,000
Mortgage Insurance	$19,000	$13,950	$11,900	$0
Total Mortgage Required	$494,000	$463,950	$436,900	$400,000
Amortization Period	25 years	25 years	25 years	25 years
Mortgage Rate	3.09%	3.09%	3.09%	3.09%
Mortgage Type	5-Year Fixed	5-Year Fixed	5-Year Fixed	5-Year Fixed
Monthly Mortgage Payment	$2,361	$2,217	$2,088	$1,912
Accelerated Biweekly Mortgage Payment	$1,180	$1,109	$1,044	$956

In the table, you can see that a larger down payment makes your mortgage payments increasingly less expensive, and while this example shows payments over a twenty-five-year amortization, if you choose to pay your mortgage off faster, the payments would be larger. All these variables affect how much you'll have to contribute over the course of your mortgage.

The simple choice to pay your mortgage biweekly rather than monthly, for example, can save you significant dollars in the long run. Let's assume you put down 10 percent as a down payment on the $500,000 house. Monthly, you'd pay $2,217, and with an accelerated biweekly plan, your payments would be $1,109 every two weeks. Here's the math:

$2,217 x 12 (monthly payments) = $26,604 (per year)
$1,109 x 26 (acceerated biweekly payments) = $28,834 (per year)
$28,834 - $26,604 = $2,230

That small difference might not seem significant, but it adds up as you stretch out the years. In our example above, paying your mortgage monthly for twenty-five years will cost you $201,181 in interest. By paying an accelerated biweekly payment, your interest costs drop to $177,141. That's a savings of over $24,000 (assuming interest rates remained constant).

That's one way to cut down how much you spend across the lifetime of your mortgage, but you can also increase your monthly payments or put down an annual lump sum right on the principal. Here's how that could play out:

- If you pay $100 more with each biweekly payment, you'll save $28,018.07 in interest over the life of your mortgage and shorten your amortization by 3.2 years! That's only $6.67 a day!
- If you pay $600 more a month, you'd save $65,423 in interest over the life of your mortgage and shorten your amortization by 7.5 years![22]

This quick number crunching is a great way to encourage savings. Call me a nerd if you'd like, but I'd even say it's exciting and addictive when you actually see the numbers in front of you. It's so satisfying to see how making small changes can add up to large savings in your favour!

Step #9: Don't Forget Other Costs

As a homeowner, you'll have to keep in mind other costs that add up quickly and that you may not have factored into your mortgage payments and overall budget.

There are the costs associated with the mortgage and house itself:

- Closing and other costs (which vary by province and city) make up a number of expenses you might not have thought of such as:
  - *Legal fees*
  - *Title insurance*
  - *Land transfer taxes*
  - *Mortgage registration*
  - *Homeowner's insurance*
  - *Mortgage application (not all lenders charge this)*
  - *Property appraisal*
  - *Federal and provincial taxes (if you're buying a new home)*
  - *Home inspection*
  - *Moving costs*
  - *Condo fees*
- Painting, flooring, and other aesthetic updates
- Appliance purchases
- Home repairs

You should also consider investing in insurance. Homeowner's insurance will protect your house and assets in the event of damages, and some insurance will even offer coverage in the event of disability or death. The bank will offer you insurance that will pay your remaining mortgage balance if you pass away—if both you and your spouse are listed on the mortgage, then it will pay your balance if you both pass away. As part of the insurance plans offered by the bank, there are also options for covering your payments if you are unable to work. You can opt in to this insurance, which is easy—it's usually done along with all the other mortgage paperwork, and there are minimal questions or extraneous requirements. However, there are some downsides to this type of insurance, including the fact that it is more expensive than a stand-alone life insurance policy.

A stand-alone life insurance policy and/or disability policy may be the better option for you if you have the time. The process is considerably more involved, but the benefits will make the effort worth it. The payments for a stand-alone policy are often less expensive than insurance offered with your mortgage, you'll have insurance tailored to your specific needs, your insurance will remain constant rather than declining as your mortgage balance does, and if you were to die, the benefits would go beyond just paying off the mortgage. Finally, because the approval process is much more in-depth, it is less common that insurers fail to make their promised payments.

As you get older, life insurance will become more expensive, so when you get a mortgage or have a major financial milestone, it is an opportune time for you and your family to review your insurance needs.

WHERE ARE THEY NOW?

Scott and Allyson got a major financial wake-up call when they both turned fifty-five. They had heard that mortgage rates were increasing and decided to dust off their mortgage paperwork. When they realized they would be seventy-five years old by the time they'd paid off their mortgage, they decided that it was time to finally become thoughtfully debt free.

Their friends had recently visited a nonprofit credit counsellor to get help paying off their own mortgage and had had a great experience, so Scott and Allyson also took the courageous leap to set up an appointment. After visiting with the counsellor, they were pleasantly surprised to hear that they were doing better than they thought. The counsellor suggested they get a consolidation loan from their bank, which combined all of their high-interest-rate credit cards into one loan payment with a much lower interest rate.

With the help of their banker, they set a five-year plan to be debt free (other than their mortgage and line of credit). By consolidating all of their debts and the combined interest they'd have to pay over the next five years, Scott and Allyson determined how much money they'd need to dedicate each day, week, and month to fast-track their payments. Once they've paid off those high-interest-rate debts, they can start to build a savings account. It's a little later in life than they had hoped, but they both plan to work past retirement.

Scott and Allyson also met with a financial professional to help them maximize their future savings. Since they are both earning a large income, they were advised to maximize their RRSPs as well as their employer plans, and then use the hefty tax refund each year to pay down their mortgage principal. This will make them mortgage free eight years sooner. They had better start planning that mortgage-burning party!

Going Solo

Parenting might be the most rewarding, demanding, and simultaneously exhausting job you'll ever have. Your return on investment can be immeasurable. And yet, there's no denying that having children is expensive. So how do you balance the joy of a growing family with the exponentially increasing debt that can come with it? What if you're doing it on a single income?

Jason has been struggling with these questions for years now. He is the lucky—and single—dad of two young kids, and as the sole breadwinner, money has always been tight for their family of three. The debts have been racking up—he's maxed out his credit cards, he's been relying heavily on his line of credit, and he hasn't even been able to start thinking about saving for his children's education.

He lives paycheque to paycheque, and has never felt financially secure enough to plan for big expenses, only paying for things as they come up. He should be setting money aside for recurring costs such as back-to-school shopping (for clothes as his children continue to grow and yearly supplies), family holidays, and extra-curricular activities. He is regularly facing cash crunches, and he falls back on expensive payday loans from lenders.

He can't keep living like this, but he can't even manage to come up for air long enough to find a solution. As alone as he might feel as a single parent, he's not the only one feeling this heavy burden. With the right tools, and a little bit of time, he can fix it and still find money to put aside for his children's future.

WHERE HE WENT WRONG

Jason wasn't planning on having to raise his kids on his own, but when his wife passed away from a sudden brain aneurysm at the age of thirty-one, he was suddenly the single father of two sons, a two-year-old and a four-year-old. They hadn't found the time to invest in life insurance before his wife died, so Jason was faced with the burden of single-income parenthood from the very beginning, with no time to think about what it would cost him.

Misstep #1: Not Crunching the Numbers

Having and raising children will have an emotional and physical toll on you, but the financial cost of raising kids can follow you long after the kids have moved away from home. The best estimate I can give you for the cost of raising a child to the age of eighteen in Canada is approximately $258,000, a figure determined by personal finance magazine *MoneySense* in 2011 and adjusted for today's inflation.[23] That number can seem intimidating, and you may have read or heard similarly high estimates for the cost of raising children today from friends and coworkers, but I caution you not to be alarmed by seeing such a high number written on the page like that. Remember, the cost will be spread out over eighteen years of your life, so it's much more manageable to think of it in terms of what you're actually shelling out each year, month, and week.

If it costs you $258,000 to raise a kid from birth to the age of eighteen, that's an annual cost of $14,333, or $1,195 monthly, per child. While I personally prefer not to go into any situation unprepared, parenthood is an endeavour where preparedness is key, and knowledge is power. Knowing where your money is going if you have children is the first step to success. The next step is planning, because you can't afford not to have a financial plan if you're going to raise them, save for their future, and keep yourself sane along the way.

Misstep #2: Relying on Payday Loans

Payday loans should always be a last resort and, preferably, not used at all. Payday loans make it easy to get your short-term needs funded quickly, and they have become dangerously effortless now that most can be completed online, with the money emailed to you within mere hours. It's important to note that these lenders are also often super friendly, easy to deal with, and provide approval faster and with fewer barriers than trying to get a bank loan, all of which is intentional. These loans are promoted as small advances—usually less than $500—and appear innocent enough, but the reality is that the interest rate and fees can amount to nearly 600 percent per year. If you don't pay them off when they're due (usually within fourteen days), the fees and interest keep compounding as they roll over. Relying on a payday loan will only put you further into debt. Ask yourself this: if you rely on these lenders for $300 in the short-term, are you likely to find or earn that same $300, plus interest, when it comes time to repay it next month? Probably not.

Whenever Jason has applied for a payday loan, he's always been desperate for cash and has assumed there wouldn't be a better option at his bank. As a single father, he also doesn't want to admit to needing help, and payday loans allow for anonymity. If you've ever felt embarrassed or ashamed about your money situation, whether you're a parent or not, you're not alone. In fact, a survey of 1,500 Canadians by the Financial Consumer Agency of Canada in 2016 revealed that 20 percent of households with an income of $80,000 or more have used a payday loan.[24]

The bad news is that payday loans continue to be common, and new shops are constantly popping up in neigbourhoods and online because it's big business for them, and big debt for you. The good news is that with a little money management, you can avoid them, because there is a very real and dangerous cost associated with this short-term solution.

Misstep #3: Buried by Debt

Jason is too focused on ensuring that he and his kids have enough food on their table and a roof over their head to devote any time to thinking about where his money is going and how he can start to save for their future, rather than just meet the needs of the moment. He is paying only the minimum payment on his loans, credit cards, line of credit, and mortgage, and he's never felt able to pay more. With the help of an online calculator, he would quickly see what a difference it would make if he were to pay just a few more dollars per month.

The cost to service debt can be a substantial burden on your bank account, and you're only padding the bank's wallet in the process. If Jason made time to calculate how much money he's losing to fees and interest, he'd be more conscious every time he goes to make a payment. Without considering his mortgage, since it's locked in at a good rate and he doesn't need to contribute more until his high-interest-rate credit card debt is paid off, here's what it currently costs for Jason to service his debt:

	Amount due	Interest Rate	Monthly Cost to Service Debt
Line of Credit	$59,000	4.45%	$219
Bank Credit Card	$15,000	18%	$225
Department Store Credit Card	$6,000	28%	$140
Payday Loan	$3,800	47.71%	$151
Total:			$735

Jason is losing $735 a month in servicing costs to pay the interest on his various loans, and not a cent of that will go to actually paying down his debt. Annually, if he doesn't contribute a large amount at any point, he stands to lose $8,820. Money that could be used to save for his children's RESP, his retirement, or maybe even a nice family vacation!

Where Are Your Payments Going?

It's important to know that when you make a monthly interest payment, it's not contributing to the repayment of a loan, as they sometimes purely cover the interest costs. With credit cards for example, your minimum payment is the interest cost plus a little extra (usually 3 percent of your outstanding balance), so by making the minimum payment—and not a dollar more—you'll pay off the card eventually, but it might take years or decades to do so. On the other hand, with a line of credit, you can pay interest-only payments. If you do so, you'll never pay it off.

I've said it before, and I'll say it again: knowledge is power when it comes to understanding how lenders are profiting from your debt, and Canadians still need to do their homework. A recent report from the Financial Consumer Agency of Canada revealed that 50 percent of people surveyed did not understand the terms and conditions of a home equity line of credit (HELOC), a line of credit where your house is collateral. The same report revealed that more than 25 percent of respondents made interest-only payments, and 62 percent of those same respondents expected to pay off their HELOC in full within five years. That's awfully optimistic, considering that more than three million Canadians with a HELOC owe an average of $65,000, not to mention the fact that if you're making interest-only payments, you won't pay off your HELOC in a lifetime, let alone within five years.[25] This is just one example of many where lenders profit from a borrower's ignorance, but now that you're backed with this knowledge, you can go off into the world and pay down those debts!

Misstep #4: Not Being Smart with a Bonus

Jason can't always manage to pay his minimum payment on his loans, so when he gets a bonus at work, he makes a lump sum payment to cover future months in advance. He assumes he's paying off his next monthly payments, but as we learned with Ian and Crystal, this is only hurting his credit score, and he'll still need to pay a minimum amount every month.

Instead of putting that extra money down on loans, Jason should be building an emergency account, because he's currently raising two sons with no extra funds to rely on if anything ever happened. Currently, if an emergency comes up, Jason depends on his credit card. He rationalizes that by contributing any extra money to his credit card, he's making room on his card if he ever needs it for an emergency. He thinks he's found a loophole, but due to his infrequent payment history, his account has been flagged.

When his uncle passed away last year, Jason got a small inheritance of $5,000, and he thought about putting it in a savings account until he realized the interest rate at his bank was under 2 percent, so it would practically just sit there. Instead, he used the money to pay down a credit card that he had maxed out at $20,000. Unfortunately, he received a terrible surprise two weeks later while doing his online banking and saw that he still didn't have any available credit on his card. When he called his bank, he learned that after his $5,000 payment, they decided to reduce the available credit for his account to $15,000 because of his spotty payment history. His emergency "account" disappeared in a flash.

Misstep #5: A House Built for Four or More

Jason and his wife bought their house when they first got married, with the intention of filling it with a family and a lifetime of memories. Since she passed a few years ago, he hasn't been ready to think about downsizing. He's paying for the mortgage all on his own, but he bought it when they still had a dual income.

Now, he can't afford his own house, but he'd prefer to stay put for the kids if he can. He still has options for offsetting the cost of the house if they don't move, but Jason has been so stressed with his finances that he hasn't even thought of how he can bring in more income. The basement of the house is semifinished, and with about $20,000 of work, he could transform it into a fully functioning rental suite. Yes, it requires putting money down upfront, but he could easily make it back within a year or two. Even if he doesn't want to rent out his basement year-round, he could consider listing it as a vacation rental through sites such as Airbnb or Vrbo.

It can be difficult to make a financial decision when things get sentimental, but try not to let your emotions cloud your judgment. There are often multiple ways to solve the problem; you just have to find the path of least resistance.

Misstep #6: Teaching Bad Habits

As a parent, Jason has the difficult task of teaching his sons all the best habits, and none of the bad ones. Currently, he's struggling to not pass on his own bad habits to his children, and he needs to correct himself before he can begin to set a good example for his sons. While constantly balancing money and other life stresses, Jason finds that he says yes to whatever the boys want, succumbing to the guilt of not being present enough for his sons, and not wanting to disappoint them. The last thing he wants his children to know is that he can't afford to spoil them.

As tempting as it may be to protect your children from the realities of your life and the world, you need to set them up for success by creating a strong financial foundation, even if that means being more open with them about the family's finances. Jason's sons are going to be in for a big surprise once they're on their own if they keep getting whatever they want, whenever they want.

If you're hoping to instill good money habits in your children, consider paying them an allowance to teach the importance of earning and saving money. Instead of pretending the problems don't exist, including your family in your financial education can make it a learning and growth opportunity for everyone.

Misstep #7: No Protection

Protecting yourself and your children for the future can be an onerous task, but it's an important one. After Jason's wife passed away without any substantial life insurance, Jason verified that he at least has insurance coverage on his mortgage, but he didn't get much further than that while grieving her death. With his monster mortgage and numerous debts, Jason isn't adequately covered if something happens to him.

Jason has some death and disability insurance through his plan at work, but he's never taken stock of the plan and whether or not it would cover funeral costs and the remaining debts at his death while still leaving enough for his children. There are many plans out there that will cover all this and more so that you can rest easy knowing you are protecting your children and their future.

THE SOLUTION?

Whether you're a single parent, parenting with a partner, or child-less, the following solutions will help you handle debt repayment, focus on the cost of your debt, know when to get help, and learn how to talk about money with the people in your life—young or old. You can take charge of your finances, and it's easiest once you know where your money is going.

Step #1: Determine Costs

Jason completed the Thirty-Day Anti-Budget and found the following five categories took up most of his disposable income:

1. Housing
2. Childcare
3. Interest on his debt
4. Food
5. Extracurricular activities for his children

How and where do you spend your disposable income? With that in mind, the following solutions can help minimize costs across all categories.

Step #2: Find Support

According to the Organisation for Economic Co-operation and Development (OECD), on average Canadian parents spend 22.2 percent of their net income on childcare. Single parents can spend up to a third of their net income on childcare annually.[26] If you're struggling to pay high childcare costs, there are alternatives.

Find ways to gain the support of other parents. Consider pooling your money together with other parents to hire a full-time nanny. If you're a low-income parent, explore government funded or subsidized childcare options in your community, as well as provincial tax benefits to help offset the costs. Beyond childcare, find moral support where you can. There are community-living housing opportunities and single parent support groups. If necessary, start your own support group at your child's school, pool shopping for groceries at wholesale stores, and carpool when you can.

Step #3: Understand the Real Costs of Payday Loans

These high-cost instant loans are becoming so common that the Canadian government is concerned that those using them don't fully understand how they work. In 2009, the Financial Consumer Agency of Canada calculated that 1.9 percent of Canadians had used a payday loan. By 2014, that figure had more than doubled to 4.3 percent,[27] and it will continue to grow unless people start to understand the real costs of relying on payday loans.

Extra charges on a $300, 14-day loan

Here's what you would be charged on top of a $300, 14-day loan from various sources.

Borrowing from a line of credit:	Overdraft protection on a bank account:	Cash advance on a credit card:	Payday loan:
$5.81	$7.19	$7.42	$63.00

In the chart above, you can see just how expensive it is to rely on payday loans when you're tight on cash, assuming the payday loan comes with a $21 fee per $100 borrowed, which was the average cost of payday loans in 2016 when the FCAC released these findings.[28] If you have been turning to these loans in your time of need, work to save preventively: Make a list of times in the year where you often use payday loans, such as holidays, birthdays, back-to-school shopping, or paying your property taxes. Put these items in your calendar and set a reminder for at least sixty days beforehand to begin saving. If saving isn't a possibility, review your borrowing options well in advance and avoid payday loans wherever you can!

Step #4: Seek Professional Help

If you're relying on credit to make ends meet, struggling to pay your minimum payments each month, and your debt is a ceaseless weight on your shoulders, you don't have to find a solution on your own. A nonprofit credit counsellor will review your debts and your best options, such as the possibility of a consolidation loan, interest relief from your creditors, a plan to pay your creditors, or referring you to a bankruptcy trustee.

When you owe money to a creditor or the government (the Canada Revenue Agency), the worst thing you can do is remain silent, because they can and will always assume the worst and take the action they deem necessary. If you open up a conversation, you can negotiate with your creditors or even have a counsellor do it on your behalf. You can also speak to your bank or credit card company to negotiate a payment schedule or reduction in your interest rate. As you now know, if you have a mortgage and are otherwise in good standing with your lender, you may be granted an annual "skip payment" option that will give you some breathing room for a month.

I understand that if you're swimming in debt, you may not be feeling confident or assured enough to call up your creditors yourself, which is when a nonprofit credit counsellor can help. They take away the shame and embarrassment, and provide the answers you need to get back on track. Your first appointment or call is free, and they'll review your credit report with you at no cost. A word of warning, though: Shop around, and be wary of any organization promising you a quick fix for repairing your credit and debt. Start with a nonprofit organization, and ask for referrals from other clients they've worked with. Getting out of debt is hard, but every step you take will build back your confidence and show you that there is a way out and a brighter path forward.

What about Consolidation Loans?

A consolidation loan can benefit someone with a lot of high-interest debt. This type of loan brings all your debt and payments together in one bigger loan with only one payee. It's a first step to debt freedom. Although the total amount might seem shocking, it's just a mental illusion. If you're consolidating high-rate credit cards and payday loans, you'll have a lower interest rate, and you'll be forced to make both interest and principal payments each month, allowing you to pay off your debt that much sooner.

If Jason consolidated all his debt with an 8 percent interest rate, he would owe $83,000 on one loan. It's true that the interest rate would be higher than the 4.45 percent rate on his line of credit, but by consolidating it all in one place, he will be forced to pay it off faster and save money on interest from his other lenders. His monthly payments will go from $1,093 to $1,699. If Jason finds an extra $600 a month from his Thirty-Day Anti-Budget results and by renting out his basement suite, he could be debt free in just over five and a half years, and save $37,964 in interest over the course of the loan.[29]

Step #5: To Avalanche or Snowball?

If you choose not to take a consolation loan or simply can't get one, you can tackle your debt in one of two ways: an "avalanche" or a "snowball" approach. With an avalanche approach, you tackle your highest-interest-rate debt first, which will net you the best return because the rate is the highest, so you stand to lose more as you prolong the repayment.

With a snowball approach, you gain momentum by paying off your smallest debt first, working toward the goal of eventually paying off your largest debt. Jason is behind on his cell phone bill by a couple of months and owes $120, and he also owes $250 on an old cable bill. Using the snowball approach, Jason can start by paying off his cell phone, which will feel rewarding, and then work on paying off his cable bill. Rinse and repeat!

No matter your approach, you must also ensure to make your minimum payments (or more) on all of your bills, on time, every month. If you can't, reach out for help.

Step #6: Find the Right Housing Solution

If you can't afford the roof over your head, you have options. You can sell and downscale to a smaller property, or you can sell, invest the profits, and rent a place if that's more affordable in your area. Of course, there can be many hidden blind spots in this onerous decision, so consider hiring a fee-only Certified Financial Planner to check your work after doing preliminary research exploring your options.

If Jason moved, he would add a costly and stressful process to an already overflowing schedule, and his two young children would have to deal with big life changes, such as the possibility of changing schools. Renting out his basement would be a more practical option and also provide the added bonus of creating a second form of revenue once he creates a livable, rentable suite. Not every option will work for you, but there is a housing solution out there that will help you rest easily at night.

Step #7: Think of Your Children

If you have children under the age of seventeen, try to budget to save for their future while managing your own financial situation if you can. If you're struggling with staying afloat among your debt, that may be the last thing on your mind, but the future you (and your children) will thank you. But there are other steps you can take to ensure that you are getting the most for your children with what you have.

As a parent, you are eligible for thousands of dollars in tax benefits each year. When filing your tax returns, be sure to claim as many of your children's expenses as possible, because currently, Canadian parents are potentially losing thousands of dollars each year by not claiming expenses. You may be eligible for any or all of the following:

1. **Childcare Expense Deduction:** Unless you have a spouse or family member who's able to provide childcare services, you probably qualify for this deduction. You're eligible if your children have a caregiver, attend nursery schools or educational camps or boarding schools, or use other childcare services.[30]
2. **Canadian Child Benefit (CCB):** This is a tax-free monthly benefit calculated based on need and your family's household income. You will receive a payment for every child under the age of eighteen, and on average families receive over $6,000 annually.[31]

3. **National Child Benefit (NCB):** The NCB supplements the CCB nicely, and if you qualify as a low-income family, you will receive monthly payments throughout the year. The NCB also allows provinces and territories to create services for low-income families within their jurisdiction.[32]

4. **Child Disability Benefit:** If you have a child under the age of eighteen with a severe and prolonged physical or mental impairment, you can be eligible for this benefit, which is also given out in monthly payments.[33]

Step #8: Determine Your Needs and Wants

You've probably thought about what your kids need, but what about what they want? How do you distinguish between the two? You can start by sitting down with your children to make a list of all the things they desire in the near future—let them be as creative as possible. This is a great exercise for you to do as well, because we so rarely take the time to think about what we want. Thinking in advance can help prevent impulse purchases for both you and your children.

Once your children have created a list, have them mark each item with an *N* (need) or a *W* (want). It might be difficult at first, but it will open up a conversation about money and how your children won't always get everything they want. I'd recommend doing this exercise every two months or so. It should only take you fifteen minutes, and your children will get better and better at editing down their wants.

Food is an obvious necessity but can also get quite costly when you're feeding a family. You can certainly save money by buying what's on sale at the grocery store, especially when buying things with a long shelf life such as toiletries, canned food, and boxed items. I hazard against buying fresh items simply because they're on sale, because food waste can cost you and the planet in the long run—in Canada alone, we waste approximately 40 percent of our food, which costs close to $31 billion a year.[34] So if you don't have a plan for all that fresh food and it's just going to sit in your fridge for two weeks before getting put in the trash, avoid it—even if it's on sale. To prevent costly food waste, try some of these strategies:

- **Develop a seasonal meal plan and menu.** As a family, record the meals you enjoy over the next month. Can you find five to seven recipes that you can circulate through for weekly meal plans? Once you've pinned them down, type out the recipes, create a grocery list for each one, and print a copy to keep in the car or in your wallet. I also like to keep a copy of my menu plan and grocery list stored on my phone for any last-minute shopping needs.
- **Don't buy perishables just because they're on sale.** If it's not part of your meal plan, don't buy it.
- **Write a weekly list of items that are close to expiring.** Paste the list on the fridge, and use it as the basis for that week's meal plan so you know what you have to use up first.

Step #9: Create a Banking System for Your Children

How do you currently talk to your children about money? Do you have rules for when and how you buy them things? If you're looking for a new approach (or any approach at all), consider a system that you can build upon as your children grow up. I've created a few guidelines for establishing a banking system for your children that over time will teach them when to spend just for fun, how to put thought into short-term desires, and how to save up for longer-term purchases. When your children are in their late teens, they can even practice using and paying back credit responsibly before getting a first credit card.

Under Five Years Old

■ Talk about: Cash! Getting your children accustomed to using and seeing cash will teach them so many math and history lessons. Have bills and coins around the house that your children can play with (under supervision—I wouldn't want anyone swallowing a coin), and keep a few pieces of foreign currency the next time you travel so you can teach your children about money from around the world.

■ Do: Get a piggy bank for your children. Whenever they receive money from an allowance or a gift, encourage your children to put it in their piggy bank so that the next time they "want" something it becomes a teachable moment when they can use their own money to purchase it. This exercise should be all about fun and the enjoyment of earning money—an element we too often forget as adults.

Ages Five to Ten

■ Talk about: Short-term goals. Are there events or outings coming up that your child can save up for and learn the merits of saving in the short-term in the process? Maybe there's a ski trip or a swim pass they've asked about. Have a discussion with your child about how much you are willing to contribute to a purchase, and ask that they save up to make the difference.

■ Do:
   • *Create a goal thermometer that they can fill in as they save toward their desire. Indicate on the chart how much you'll contribute to their goal.*

- *Find ways for your children to earn extra income. Can they hold a garage sale to sell their unused toys, or help at home by cleaning the yard?*
- *Create a second piggy bank for this short-term savings goal. When they make money, help your child allocate the funds between their spending bank and their savings bank.*

Ages Ten to Fifteen

■ Talk about: Long-term goals. Right now, the future might hold a school trip to Europe, but how do they break down that savings goal into monthly and weekly goals? Again, discuss how much you are willing to contribute to the purchase, and help your child calculate how much they will have to earn on their own.

■ Do:

- *Help your children find ways to earn money inside and outside of the house. Are there families in your neighbourhood with young children who need babysitters?*
- *Create another goal thermometer for your child's long-term goals if they still need the visual reminder. At this point, your children should be learning how to split their money into three pots: fun savings; short-term savings (like an adult saving up for new clothes, a fridge, or a vacation); and long-term savings (like an adult saving up for retirement).*
- *Create a third piggy bank, or consider opening an official bank account for your child. Encourage them to save toward this long-term goal in the account. It's a great opportunity for them to see a physical branch, learn how to check their balance online, and watch their funds grow in their account.*

Ages Fifteen to Eighteen

- ■ Talk about: Credit cards! It's important to start the discussion early about the importance of credit and paying off the charges in full each and every month, as well as the consequences of not making payments on time.
- ■ Do: Create a mock credit card system for your teen. Determine how much credit you will grant them, the parameters for paying it back, and if there will be a financial penalty for not paying it back. If you're shopping with your child and they see something they want to buy but can't afford, consider granting them credit, and try to mimic the real experience as much as possible. At the age of sixteen, your children can even start applying for summer and part-time jobs.

Step #10: Get Adequately Insured

There are so many different types of life insurance on the market that I could dedicate an entire chapter to going through them all, but I won't bore you with the details. If you do have a lot of debt, I'd suggest you take the time to examine your insurance needs with a professional, whether that's a Certified Financial Planner or an insurance broker. I recognize that it can be difficult to justify the cost of paying for life insurance when you're trying to tackle debt, but that's precisely when your family is the most vulnerable. Plus, if you apply for life insurance when you're young and healthy, you'll face lower payments.

According to a recent study, 63 percent of Canadians have some form of insurance, but less than one-third of Canadians have insurance that covers unforeseen life events, which raises the question: Do you have enough coverage to protect you and your family from death and disability?[35] If you're not sure, make visiting a professional a priority on your list of financial action items.

WHERE IS HE NOW?

Jason and his sons are learning how to be more money smart as a family. As a father, Jason has made it a priority to start talking more openly about money with his children, and he's even started a piggy bank for each son where they can learn how to save and earn money on their own.

There are too many memories in the house to sell it right now, so Jason did his homework and determined that renovating and renting out his basement suite is the most cost-effective way to keep it but still offset some of the costs of living there. He's reached out to some renovators, all of whom estimate the renovations will cost approximately $20,000. Using his bank's online calculator, Jason discovered that he can get a loan with an 8 percent interest rate, which he can pay back with monthly payments of $405.54 over five years. Once the renovations are done, Jason will be able to rent out the basement for $1,100/month, which will net a monthly cash inflow of $694.47.

Determined to become financially stable for both himself and his children's future, Jason also invested in a financial professional who crunched a few more numbers for him. Together, they learned that he has $43,000 in unused RRSP room. If he takes out a loan for $43,000 to fund his RRSP, he could expect a tax refund next year of approximately $20,627 because he is in a marginal tax bracket of 47.97 percent as an Ontario resident.[36] The interest on an RRSP loan can be as low as 4.8 percent, which would be much less than a traditional loan, and his monthly payment to repay the loan would be $807.53 a month over five years.

Now Jason is netting $292.47 a month from his basement rental once he's paid his RRSP loan and is growing a $43,000 pot of money that will be available for his retirement. With the right investments, his $43,000 could easily become over $76,000 over the next twenty years, even with conservative ones. With these two simple steps, Jason is already feeling more confident about being able to raise his sons in a financially stable and confident household. Plus, he's going to continue to teach his sons good money sense so that they can all feel good about money.

The Sandwich Generation

Have you heard of the sandwich generation? It's a term that's been coined to refer to a generation of people who are sandwiched between the responsibilities of caring for both their parents and their own children. It's become a reality for many people as our parents age beyond the ability to care for themselves, and the financial and emotional burden falls to the children as they pick up the pieces. Thankfully, there are steps you can take to help alleviate the struggle to find both time and money for your extended family.

For Lauren and Rob, a married couple with full-time jobs and two children, life was very busy before Rob's mother began showing signs of early onset dementia and a host of physical ailments. Rob is a captain with Air Canada and Lauren runs a PR firm, and both juggle the tasks of running the household while attending as many soccer games and dance rehearsals as they can. They're a real success in so many ways—they have zero consumer debt, their mortgage will be paid off by the time they're sixty, and they save 15 percent of their income. Unfortunately, Rob hadn't been preparing for his mother's health to deteriorate, and they're going to have to dip into their savings to help cover the medical costs. Their financial plan has been thrown off, and they're emotionally and physically exhausted.

WHERE THEY WENT WRONG

Lauren and Rob have done well to stay on top of their debt while still allocating enough for their various activities as well as savings. Unfortunately, a hard reality is the fact that they should have considered their aging parents as factors in their financial strategies. With the right planning and adjustments, Lauren and Rob can save both time and money while ensuring they still have time to enjoy the life they've built together.

Misstep #1: Underestimating the Value of Time

With busy work and social calendars, Lauren and Rob have practically scheduled their entire life down to the minute. They recognize that time is precious, which became all too obvious when Rob's mom fell sick, but they've never considered that their time has worth. As a family of four with a dual income from stable and well-paying jobs, they can afford not to do everything themselves, but they've never thought of hiring out some of their regular tasks. If they keep going at this rate, they'll be too exhausted to enjoy any of the free time that they manage to find. In order to figure out if they can afford to hire help, they must first examine the value and scarcity of their time.

Misstep #2: Trying to Do It All

As Lauren and Rob begin to reassess how they spend their time and money, they need to look at their highly scheduled lives to find opportunities to reclaim lost time. We all have so many responsibilities in a given week and only so much time to address them all. Whether it's laundry, groceries, piano lessons, or a gym class, your weekly activities likely bring you varying degrees of joy or satisfaction, so how do you prioritize the things that you both have to and want to do each week?

Misstep #3: Carrying the Burden Alone

Even before Rob's mom got sick, he and Lauren should have had a family meeting with their children to openly and honestly discuss everyone's expectations for what is and isn't possible, with both cost and time in mind. Involving everyone in family decisions ensures that no one feels left out, and creates an opportunity for compromises and priorities that everyone can agree on. Maybe Rob and Lauren don't have to attend every game and practice for the kids. Now that they are older, the kids could ease their parents' driving responsibilities by taking an Uber or Lyft, or carpooling to activities with friends. As they get closer to sixteen, they'll also have to discuss driving lessons and the possibility of contributing to the cost of a used car. Although it seemed as if Rob and Lauren had everything under control in their life, they were doing too much—to the point of nearly collapsing at the first sign of trouble. By fostering an open discussion about expectations and responsibilities, you can create a support system that is there to catch you when you need it most.

Once you've built that initial support system, consider bringing your extended family into a larger discussion about familial expectations to avoid one person having to carry all of the emotional and or financial burden of caring for a loved one. Rob should have talked with his siblings—as a preemptive discussion before their mom fell ill or once they'd learned of her dementia—to create a plan for any family emergencies. Instead, since both his sister and brother are out of province, they feel no obligation to come into the city to see what he's dealing with, and neither contribute financially to their mother's care. Whenever Rob mentions to his siblings that they should consider looking for a retirement home or assisted-living facility for their mom, they suggest that she can't afford it, but really they are worried it will eat up their inheritance. If Rob and Lauren have to cover all of the costs alone, it's best for them to know that from the beginning, rather than having to deal with that stress on top of everything else.

Misstep #4: Hiding from Their Problems

Rob hasn't talked to his mom about her health or how she wants to handle her ongoing care—including how they'll pay for it. He's always been apprehensive about talking with his mom about money and her health, as both are taboo subjects in their family. He's also convinced that she'll be reluctant to leave her house because she and Rob's dad lived there for decades, but he hasn't had the courage to ask about it. Unfortunately, as her health continues to deteriorate, he'll need to know how to proceed, and he won't always be able to get her opinion.

Misstep #5: Missed Tax Deductions

Lauren and Rob never took the time to talk to an accountant to find out if they can claim some of the money they're spending to take care of Rob's mom. The costs are quickly adding up as they

fix things around her house, cover snow removal and lawn maintenance, drive her to appointments, and provide occasional meals
and groceries. There are likely some tax deductions that will save
them money in the end, but they never thought to check.

Misstep #6: Not Planning for Their Own Future

If you haven't taken the time to think about your own health and
issues that will arise later in life, you're not alone in avoiding the
topic, but you really should take the time to address it. Lauren
and Rob avoided it until they came face-to-face with the reality of
watching Rob's mom get sick. As Rob can't take time off work easily, he heavily depends on Lauren to be the primary caregiver for
the kids and for his mom. If Lauren were to get sick or become disabled, it could drastically affect the family's finances. Thankfully,
disability and life insurance policies can protect families in such
cases, but you have to take the time to make those investments
with your future in mind.

THE SOLUTION?

No matter how much money we all make, time is the great
equalizer—we all get only the same twenty-four hours in a day.
How are you using that time, and how much satisfaction and joy do
you get during your free time? With a little bit of planning, I think
you'll find more time for the things you want to be doing.

Step #1: Discover What Your Time Is Worth

You can always find ways to make more money, but your valuable
time on this earth is finite. Once you discover what your time is

worth, you'll have a better sense of whether you are spending your time wisely. You can break down how much money you make per hour at your job, but have you also considered breaking down what your household hourly time is worth?

Let's do some quick math using the average Canadian income of $50,000 a year, or $100,000 for a household with two full-time working adults:

MONTHLY INCOME:

$$\frac{\$50,000}{12 \text{ months}} = \$4,166.67 \text{ per month}$$

WEEKLY INCOME:

$$\frac{\$4,166.67}{4 \text{ weeks}} = \$1,041.67 \text{ per week}$$

HOURLY INCOME:

$$\frac{\$1,041.67}{40 \text{ work hours}} = \$26.01 \text{ per hour}$$

In a dual-income household, the hourly wage for the family is roughly $52. What's your time worth?

Step #2: Run a One-Week Time Audit

A time audit is a study or intake of your time and how you're spending it. It'll let you see what is taking up your time and if there are alternatives you can take to regain some of that lost time. For Lauren and Rob, the following major activities are taking up most of their time outside of work and fun activities:

Task	Responsibility?	Level of frustration	Time cost	Cost of Alternative Options
Grocery shopping for the house	Lauren	Moderate	(5 minutes driving to the store + 20 minutes shopping + 5 minute driving back home) x twice a week = 1 hour/ week	Have your groceries delivered: $10-$15/ week.
Grocery shopping and delivery for Rob's mom	Lauren	High	(5 minute driving to the store + 20 minutes shopping + 15 minute driving to Rob's mom's house + 20 minute driving home) x twice a week = 2 hours/ week	Have her groceries delivered. $10-$15/ week.
Food prep for the house	Lauren and the kids	Moderate	(10 minutes whenever they find the time) x 6 times a week = 1 hour/ week	Purchase a meal-kit delivery service: $100-$200/week. Create a rotating schedule of 5 to 7 meals that the family agrees on. Designate Sunday afternoons for the kids to help with meal prep and lunches for the week.

Task	Responsibility?	Level of frustration	Time cost	Cost of Alternative Options
Food prep for Rob's mom	Lauren and Rob	High	1 hour+/week	Buy healthy frozen alternatives, and provide clear reheating instructions. $30/week. Purchase a hot meal delivery service for a few meals per week. $50/week. Order meals for her once or twice a week using a food delivery app such as Skip the Dishes or Uber Eats. $50/week.
Laundry for the house	Lauren and the kids	Moderate	1 hour+/week	Create a schedule for the kids to help with laundry. $0. Set up free dry cleaning pickup and delivery for Lauren's and Rob's work clothes. Delivery = $0. Dry cleaning = $50/week.
Laundry for Rob's mom	Lauren	High	20 minutes driving to the house + 2 hours to complete loads + 20 minutes to fold and put away + 20 minutes driving home = 3 hours/week.	Hire a house cleaner once a week who will also do Rob's mom's laundry and bedding. ~$50/week. Research provincial programs that will provide services for free or at a subsidized rate for seniors. $0-$20/week.

Task	Responsibility?	Level of frustration	Time cost	Cost of Alternative Options
Lawn/snow care at the house	Rob and the kids	Moderate	2–3 hours/month	Pay the kids $25/month and set a clear schedule for the task.
Lawn/snow care at Rob's mom's house	Rob	High	2–3 hours/month	$200/month for snow removal $150/month for lawn care
Driving Rob's mom to the doctor and other outings	Rob and Lauren	Low	4–5 hours/week	Rob and Lauren love spending time with his mom, but her medical appointments are time-consuming. Hire a senior driving service that can be used for some doctors' appointments. $50/week. Hire a senior care provider (often offered by provincial government) that will pick up Rob's mom and take her to programs at a retirement facility, or for other outings.
Family dinners	Lauren	Low	7–10 hours/week	With grocery delivery, food prep Sundays, the kids' involvement, and preset menu plans, the family can avoid fast food and an overreliance of ordering take-out. Save time and money!

Task	Responsibility?	Level of frustration	Time cost	Cost of Alternative Options
Housecleaning	Lauren and teach the kids	High	3–5 hours/week	Hire a cleaner a few times a month. $200-$400/month
Driving kids to practice	Lauren and Rob	Moderate	3 hours/week	Order an Uber or Lyft for some practices. $40/week. Calculate the cost of paying for driving lessons and a used car in exchange for the kids driving themselves around. Organize a carpool schedule with the other parents to alleviate some of the driving.
Driving kids to friends' places, movies, etc.	Lauren and Rob	Low	2 hours/week	Lauren and Rob love the quality time they get with their kids while driving them around town. No change necessary!

Using this table as a guide, reassess how you are spending your time each week. It's a useful activity not only for discovering where the time goes, but also how much enjoyment or frustration you get from it and if there is the possibility of redistributing some of the work load.

Step #3: Consider the Cost of Help

After running a time audit, it should be clear to you by now that your time has value. Of course, if you're at a point in your life where you are still trying to make sure you have enough at the end of every month to pay your rent and feed yourself, then hiring extra help probably isn't a priority for you right now. Hopefully, if you're reading this book, you're looking for ways to get control of your finances and build yourself up to a point where you can afford to pay for extra help. When that time comes, remember this advice: Sometimes, it makes more sense to spend money, and not time, on household tasks.

If you hypothetically earn $35/hour, and the chore of cleaning your house is a weekly three hours you dread, the cost of hiring a house cleaner for $25/hour might be worth it to save you the stress alone. It's true that you're not making $35/hour while cleaning your house, but with a free hour, you could be earning that money on your own time. Maybe you can take an extra shift, put in more hours at work, or spend more time marketing yourself if you're self-employed to invest in making more money in the future. And if you're able, sometimes it's worth buying time to be able to spend doing more of what you enjoy.

Step #4: Hold a Family Meeting

However you define family—whether it's a combination of roommates, offspring, spouse, siblings, or your own independence as a family of one—make the time to talk about financial and household responsibilities. A family meeting doesn't have to be extensive and will look different depending on the family. The main objective is to log issues surrounding financial and time constraints, as well as agreements on how to fix it. While the best-laid plans can fall apart, you do need a plan to begin with.

Once you've created a list of weekly tasks for your household using the time audit grid, you'll be armed and ready for a family meeting. You can demonstrate to your family how the tasks are currently distributed, which will enable a discussion about how you can redistribute the tasks—whether that's by having your children take on more responsibilities or by hiring help when you're able. If you have children, as they get older, they can take on more and more responsibilities.

Again, if you're able, consider paying your children an allowance for their help with the chores. When children make their own money from an allowance, they become more conscious when spending that money. If your children get an allowance for doing certain chores—such as cleaning their room or washing the dishes after dinner—then you could consider giving them an additional financial incentive when you ask them to do something extra such as spring cleaning the yard. Earning extra money for extra work can prepare them for adulthood—as they find more work and do a good job, they can continue to make more money. It can also help them to reach their extracurricular goals (going on a ski trip or to a concert).

A family meeting can go many ways, but by the end of meeting, I hope you have a plan for distributing the work. If you live alone, that might mean hiring help or just making a schedule for yourself that distributes your chores throughout an entire month so that it feels manageable. If you live with a partner or roommates, it might look like each of you is claiming the chores that cause you the least amount of frustration and stress. Most importantly, I hope you are able to reclaim some of your lost time!

Step #5: Open up the Conversation

For many families, the burden of eldercare often falls to one child, even if there are other siblings in the picture, but this can lead to emotional, mental, and financial burnout. While dealing with the stress of an ill or aging parent, you likely won't find the time to right this imbalance, so it's best to prepare preemptively for the situation. If you do find yourself in the middle of this situation, consider setting up a family meeting with your extended family. It doesn't have to be in person if your family is scattered around the globe. Consider speaking via Skype or by phone if that's the best possible option. You may also wish to hire an advocate—such as a financial professional, lawyer, accountant, a social worker if your parent is already in the health system, or a counsellor from a retirement home—to guide this meeting if you suspect it will cause a fight within your family. These professionals can help give you the confidence, statistics, and structure for a thoughtful conversation with the rest of your family while addressing major issues.

Rob's brother and sister are in denial that their mother is really sick, and they are selfishly worried about losing some of their inheritance if she moves into a pricey retirement home. With the help of an advocate, Rob could explain to his siblings that there's a financial benefit to moving their mother to a retirement residence. As a resident of Alberta, she would qualify for several senior benefits and allowances to help supplement the costs of her care. There are also provincial benefits available if Rob's mother insists on staying in her home. However, they should consider the potential improvement in her quality of life if she were to move to a retirement home, namely because she will not face the isolation of aging alone at home.

Ideally, Rob's siblings would put their mother's needs before their own selfish desires without the help of a monitored family meeting, but that isn't always the case. By including everyone in the discussion, Rob can feel like he's making the right decision to move his mother into a retirement residence, which may not be as expensive as they had all imagined and will free up Lauren and Rob's schedule to spend more quality time with his mother once they're not overburdened by looking after her house.

Step #6: Talk about the Future

There is no easy way to talk to a parent about their health issues, decreasing independence, or eventual death. Unfortunately, it's a reality we'll all face, and if you can manage it, having the conversation sooner rather than later will benefit you in the long run.

Since Rob's mother is already suffering from dementia, they'll have to have the conversation over time while she's lucid, until she gets the full picture of what's being asked of her. It'll be a hard adjustment for her after having lived in their family home for several decades, but Rob and Lauren can open the conversation by providing her with information on the risks of falls at home and the health benefits of increased socialization. As she comes around to the idea, Rob and Lauren can take her to visit a retirement residence for a bridge game, lunch, and facility tour so she can see that she'd be living in a fun and lively environment that promotes a healthy, active lifestyle. Finally, Rob and Lauren can bring a Realtor over to get an estimate for the value of her house if she does decide to move out.

If they do choose to sell the house, Rob and Lauren can bring in a fee-only Certified Financial Planner who can assess what they should do with the money from the sale—it shouldn't just sit in a savings account earning nothing, but it also shouldn't be invested in anything risky where the principal could be lost. Ideally, the money should be invested to provide a long-term return that would offset some of the retirement residence costs. A financial pro can also advise them about the provincial support and tax credits that are available for Rob's mother.

At the end of the process, Rob and Lauren might be pleasantly surprised that she won't outlive her money by moving into a retirement residence, and it could in fact prolong her life and ease some of the pressure that Rob and Lauren have been dealing with. When you don't feel prepared to have an abrupt conversation about money with anyone in your family, taking small steps and actions can help spark a more organic conversation that unfolds over time.

Planning for Eldercare

For Yourself and Your Parents

There are several things to think about when planning for the future—whether it's for you or a loved one. I could spend a whole book writing about financial literacy for seniors, but that's not what this is, so instead, here is a crash course.

The dos and don'ts of financial planning for eldercare:

- **DO** talk to your parent about getting a Power of Attorney (POA) so you can more easily handle their financial affairs on their behalf if necessary.
  - This will allow you to make financial decisions on your parent's behalf, and it's a low-cost document that can be filed with a lawyer. It's also a good idea for a lawyer to make the decision that your parent is of sound mind when they agree to hand over this type of control. Many banks will have their own form as well, which may suffice for more minor needs such as paying bills.
  - A POA is someone that can act on your behalf while you're alive, but the minute you pass away, their power ceases. After you pass away, your executor steps in to help handle your estate. They can be the same person, but they don't have to be. Also, if you're named executor and don't feel you have the capacity to perform the required tasks, you can assign a trust company to take over your responsibilities.
- **DO** look into getting a line of credit on behalf of your parent with their bank if they can't sell their home but need to entire a retirement residence. If your parent can't or just isn't willing to sell their house to fund their care, this may be a viable option.

- **DO** find out how much your parents are eligible for in Canadian Pension Plan (CPP) payments during their lifetime to help offset long-term care costs and their death benefit. Many people are unpleasantly surprised to find themselves on the hook for costs after their parent's death if they realize too late that the estate only received a portion of the maximum amount because their parent didn't fully pay into their CPP.
- **DO** consider buying life insurance, which can cover:
  - Final expenses such as debts
  - Taxes from the sale of rental properties, stocks, Registered Retirement Savings Plans (RRSPs), or Registered Retirement Income Fund (RRIFs)
  - Tax-free gifts to family members or friends
  - Tax-free gifts to charities
- **DON'T** be ignorant about the different types of insurance. Here are just a few types of insurance that might be useful to you and your loved ones:
  - Disability insurance: Covers you while you're alive in the event you become disabled and cannot work. Do read the fine print though as disability insurance has many clauses that may make the coverage useless.
  - Long-term care: Covers you in the event you have to enter a private or public long-term care facility.
  - Critical illness (CI) insurance: Pays out a lump sum in the event that you suffer an illness set forth in your policy coverage, such as a heart attack, stroke, or cancer. This insurance ideally should be bought in your twenties or thirties, when your health is at its peak and the insurance is, therefore, less expensive. The great thing about this coverage is that it pays you a lump sum so you can do with it as you please—like travel the world in your final days or pay for experimental treatments. If you pass away before the lump sum is paid out, many policies return the premiums you've paid to your beneficiaries, so it's fairly low-risk coverage.

- **DON'T** leave the burden of planning a funeral to your children or partner. If you know what funeral arrangements you'd like after you pass away, leave detailed instructions for your family. You can even arrange for a prepaid funeral if you can afford it.
- **DO** let your POA know that you've assigned them the power to act on your behalf regarding financial decisions. Let them know where you keep the document.
- **DON'T** keep your POA document in your safety deposit box. If you do, your POA won't have proof that they're able to act on your behalf unless you give them a copy of your box key. If you do, ensure you trust that person 100 percent with the contents of your box.
- **DO** create a will as far in advance as possible. If your financial situation is complex, or you have a dependent child or family member to provide for, getting the professional advice and guidance of an estate lawyer is well worth the investment. You can always amend your will as needed.
- **DO** create personal health care directives in case of emergency. This may be another difficult one to process, but it's important to list your preferences for things such as resuscitation and comfort care, and to designate a personal agent to uphold your choices.
- **DO** keep a do-not-resuscitate notice in the car, on the fridge, or any place a person might suffer a health episode if that's a wish of your aging parent. If this document is tucked away and 911 is called, the ambulance attendant won't see it, and it's always their first measure to provide resuscitation in the event of an emergency.

Step #7: Make the Most of It

According to a new poll, Canadians contribute an average $430/ month to care for aging or ill family members, and if you're caring for more than one aging parent, this figure would be much higher.[37] Shockingly, the study also found that only 43 percent of respondents were aware of tax credits that are available to facilitate caregiving—such as the medical expense tax credit, the Canada caregiver credit, the home accessibility tax credit, and the disability tax credit—and just 12 percent of respondents were taking advantage of them. It really does pay to be informed.

If you're caring for aging parents or other loved ones, either hire a qualified accountant or start doing your own research to find out which of the following benefits you qualify for:

- tax credits
- government benefits
- disability insurance
- long-term care insurance
- Critical illness (CI) insurance
- Canadian Pension Plan (CPP) and death benefits

WHERE ARE THEY NOW?

Rob knew he needed to have the conversation with his mom about her isolation and care, but he didn't know where to start. He interviewed a few financial planners, and they told him to start with a couple of site visits to retirement residences in her local area. He booked some appointments and took her along, and he was pleasantly surprised to see that she loved one—they were both served lunch, they watched a Tai Chi class happening that afternoon, and she was even paired up with a buddy to have tea with later in the week. Rob and his mom could finally see her living outside of her house.

Later that week, he and his mom sat down with a fee-only Certified Financial Planner that specializes in long-term care and retirement planning. Together, they found out that Rob's mom was so worried about running out of money and leaving a legacy for her children that she didn't think she could afford to live in a retirement residence. The financial professional crunched some numbers, and to everyone's happy surprise, the move was more affordable than they thought. An appraiser estimated that she can sell her house for at least $500,000, and she can invest that in a low-risk portfolio of Guaranteed Investment Certificates (GICs) and bonds at her bank. If those earn 3 percent, she'll make an extra $15,000 a year, or $1,250 a month. Combined with her CPP and Old Age Security (OAS), Rob's mom will have quite enough income to offset the estimated costs of living in the retirement home.

Now that Rob and Lauren have freed up considerable time by not having to help maintain his mom's house, they have more quality time to visit with her. Every Sunday, their groceries get delivered in the morning, and the kids help with the food prep in the afternoon. Together, they make a family meal to bring over to see Rob's mom for a weekly family visit over supper.

The family has also found ways to use their time more wisely. The kids have been doing the laundry as promised, and the family has a housekeeper in twice a month. Rob realized that he likes spending the time outdoors to maintain the lawn and doing snow removal, so they didn't hire anyone to do those chores. Uber and Lyft have been a welcome relief for transporting the kids to and from practices, which should tide them over until their eldest earns enough money on his own to pay for car insurance and get his driver's license. Overall, their family life is running smoothly. Everyone knows their roles and responsibilities, and they all feel they have a renewed sense of ease and more quality time with each other.

10

The Pandemic and Business Ownership

Thirty-two percent of Canadians say they'd like to be their own boss, 20 percent want to open a small business in the next five years, and 77 percent of Canadians have wanted to be their own boss for some time.[38] While there are countless perks to opening your own shop and breaking free from the nine-to-five, there are many risks that you have to plan for. Here's a short list:

- Not earning a profit for months or years
- Using personal guarantees and debt to start your venture
- Lacking benefits and safety nets along the way

Jenna was set to have her best year ever. Her social media consultancy business was finally turning a profit and for the first time, she even had a few dollars left each month in her bank account. It's expensive living in downtown Vancouver, and she added to those costs by paying for a shared workspace for herself and her team. Since she saves money by walking to work and not owning a car, she splurges on nights out with friends and expensive concerts (far too often). She uses her credit card to finance her fun. Why not, right? Life is short, after all.

When COVID-19 hit, she was totally thrown for a loop. As companies shut down and closed their doors to the public, they slashed their social media budgets. Jenna went from dreams of a prosperous year to the immediate reality that she might not be able to afford the roof over her head when rent was due next month. Regrettably, she had to lay off all her employees, except one who was willing to work on a drastically reduced income. It was the hardest decision of her life and career. She knew people relied on their employment to keep food on the table for themselves and their families.

WHERE SHE WENT WRONG

It's not Jenna's fault that COVID forced her business to come to a screeching halt. But there were things she could have done to create a financial buffer for herself and her business. I always say that one of the first costs to consider if you're going into business is the cost of a savings plan. You don't just need a rainy-day fund for yourself but for your company and to cover payroll. Cash flow is always king when you own a small business.

Misstep #1: No Emergency Savings

Jenna made a crucial mistake as a business owner. Financial experts agree that you should have three to six months of your annual income in a safe bank account in case something goes wrong. She didn't have that rainy-day fund saved. And with COVID, it not only poured, it flooded! Many millennials and Gen Zers haven't been in the workforce long enough to have amassed a disaster fund. When COVID struck, this meant many young people had to go deeper into debt to survive the crisis.

As discussed in the introduction, you'll remember the study about the level of income needed to feel financially secure. With each $10,000 income increase, people feel exponentially more stable, but at $75,000, that levels off. And each additional boost doesn't provide any further reassurance. A new study, however, has flipped that logic on its head. COVID has frighteningly revealed that it's not your income—which for many is fleeting—that offers the best financial cushion, but your buffers and coffers. In other words, it's your savings that help you sleep at night.

Misstep #2: Carrying Lots of High-Interest-Rate Debt

Jenna never really thought about the terrifying magic of compound interest. After all, if you save in a bank account or GIC at your bank, you receive a paltry one or two percentage points. What's the incentive in that? Racking up nonessentials (wants) on a high-interest-rate credit card is easy to do but crazy when you do the math. The interest rates, usually between 11 to 29 percent, are incredibly high. That's why credit cards are so lucrative for banks and so horrible for our finances. Jenna carried a $10,000 balance on one credit card at 19.99 percent and another $6,000 on a 29 percent interest card. She paid the minimum monthly amounts of $300 and $180 respectively. But when COVID hit, she missed a few payments, went over limit, and faced hefty penalties as a result. She didn't realize she could call up her credit card companies for deferrals and instead hurt her credit by missing payments. She also didn't read her credit card statement, which said that because she missed one payment on her 19.99 percent interest rate credit card, her rate was increased to 26 percent until she made six months of payments on time!

My best advice to you? Don't be Jenna! Avoid consumer debt in the first place. If you use a credit card, pay off the balance in full every month. Don't ever think about paying the minimum and hoping that there are only sunny days ahead. Prepare for the worst if you want to stay out of debt and stress less. Think about that $480 in interest payments Jenna was paying just to keep afloat. That cash could have gone a long way to funding her personal and corporate emergency accounts.

Misstep #3: Hefty Rent Costs

Waking up to a gorgeous downtown view sounds like a dreamy goal. But not if that apartment is breaking your budget. Housing and transportation are two of the highest expenses Canadians face, so looking to those categories for reductions can have you sleeping sounder at night and fretting less about your money.

During COVID, rents have gone down in many urban centres. But guess what? Jenna has signed a contract and is stuck paying more than market value. She's also stuck downtown, when it's not the safest place to be in the pandemic. It doesn't help that it can take her over a half hour to get out of the building due to a slow elevator and new social distancing rules.

Again, this misstep isn't Jenna's fault, but renters really have been left out in the cold during COVID. If you owned your home and your mortgage was in good standing, you could skip one mortgage payment per year without penalty (without asking your banker—this has always been a standard feature of most mortgages) or you could apply to receive payment deferrals of up to six months. (The Canadian Bankers Association states that 90 percent of customers asking for a mortgage deferral were approved.)

Not so for most renters. Jenna's two-bedroom downtown Vancouver apartment sets her back $3,700 each month. Jenna justified the high rent because of the common rooms, state-of-the-art gym, and stunning views. However, without a rainy-day fund to bail her out when her income tanked, her landlord only allowed her to defer two months of rent. When she couldn't come up with rent after that, not to mention the arrears she owed, she got evicted.

Misstep #4: Bursting-at-the-seams Business Costs and No Corporate Credit

When you're an entrepreneur, cash flow is king, but almost always, cash is in short supply. Jenna had a fancy shared workspace and was staffed heavily even before the crisis. She also signed a two-year lease with her workspace. She doesn't yet realize it, but by walking away from the contract, she's still liable for those costs.

She never tried to establish corporate credit in her business name because she didn't think she could and wasn't organized with her expenses. A business line of credit could have helped her keep her space, avoid a possible lawsuit, and maybe even keep some of her staff. Many times she'd pay business costs with her personal debit card or even take a cash advance on her credit card to partially cover payroll during lean months.

Misstep #5: Forgetting That the Government Will Come Calling

Jenna, like 8.5 million plus Canadians, collected CERB (the Canadian Emergency Response Benefit) from March 2020 (when it was launched to help people who lost their jobs or income sources because of COVID-19) until September 2020. In total, she received $14,000 in income from the benefit. Because Canadians could still earn up to $1,000 a month while receiving the emergency benefit, Jenna was able to keep serving some of her clients. From the start of the year until March, her income was nearly $6,500 (gross) a month, so by September, her income totalled $40,500, including the CERB payment. She didn't put one dollar of her CERB funds away for taxes. And what she put away to pay for her GST/HST, she used to pay for her rent.

When you're traditionally employed, your employer withholds some of your pay for taxes. It means less in your hands but a welcomed nudge to make sure you don't have a hefty tax bill come April each year. If you received CERB or any other taxable government benefit, you have to estimate what your provincial and federal tax will be for the year and set those dollars aside.

At the very least, Jenna should have taken 20 percent of her CERB funds and put it away in an account for tax time.

Misstep #6: Buying Credit Card Insurance That Didn't Pay Out

You may actually have expensive insurance protection on your credit cards and loans without realizing it. When you apply for credit, it's often encouraged by the lender to opt in for insurance coverage, which is supposed to pay your minimum monthly payment when you can't (because of job loss or disability) or the entire balance in the event that you die. However, the fine print is loaded with exclusions, and in Jenna's case, she didn't qualify when she needed the coverage the most. Those wasted dollars over a decade could have been used to save up or pay down the balance on the card. When Jenna signed up for her credit card more than ten years ago, she, like most consumers, never read the fine print and has paid for something that isn't even helpful to her.

Misstep #7: Silence Isn't Golden When You Can't Pay

Millions of Canadians, through no fault of their own, lost their jobs during COVID or had their income severely disrupted. Perhaps they weren't on solid financial ground before the crisis, but with a steady paycheque, they were able to make ends meet. Maybe you found yourself in the same situation. It's incredibly hard to feel strong, confident, and proactive when you've suffered a financial blow. Calling up your bank, credit card company, or utility company to ask for help or a deferral can seem overwhelming. But by not making the calls, your creditors don't know you need help and will make decisions that are not in your favour.

What happens when you can't pay all of your bills? Which ones should you pay, and which can you be late on with minimal damage to your way of life and credit score? When the going got rough, Jenna opted to pay her cable bill and rent, but she ended up getting her cell phone cut off, which was her only lifeline to friends, family, and the few clients she had.

Misstep #8: Cashing in RRSPs Before Retirement

Registered Retirement Savings Plans (RRSPs) are meant to be used for retirement. If you cash them in during your working years, you're penalized heavily. Jenna was shocked to find out that when she cashed in $6,000 of her registered savings, she received far less in her hands.

You can actually take out your RRSPs during your working years without paying tax if you do so under two plans. The Home Buyers' Plan (HBP) for first-time home buyers allows you to take out $20,000 from your RRSP. You have fifteen years to pay yourself back. Or, if you're continuing your education with a qualifying post-secondary institution, through the Lifelong Learning Plan (LLP) you may borrow from your retirement savings as well. With this option you can also take out $20,000 from your RRSP, to be paid back in ten years.

When Jenna took out $6,000 from her RRSP, she actually only received $4,800 in her hands. As Jenna's withdrawal didn't fall under either of the allowable withdrawal categories, she has to pay tax on her withdrawal. Also, her RRSP room is now lost forever. Remember from chapter 3, when we dug into RRSPs, how you learned that each year, based on how much you earned, you had RRSP room open up (18 percent of your earned income). If you don't use the room you have each year, you can carry it forward and invest and use it in a more advantageous year. However, when you cash out your RRSP for emergency savings, you can't put that money back and you lose that opportunity for tax deferred savings growth.

Misstep #9: Expensive Lifelines

In the US, there are more payday lenders than McDonald's or even Starbucks has locations. They're on every other street corner in every major city. It's not much different here in Canada. Payday lenders are proliferating at an alarming rate. The predatory nature of these lenders has caught the attention of local and federal governments, but it hasn't helped stop their growth. In 2018, the City of Toronto stopped issuing the necessary permits for such lenders to open up shop. The unintended result? Many simply went online. This trend started well before COVID-19.[39]

When Jenna couldn't pay her rent, she resorted to an online lending service that charged her nearly 400 percent annual interest on her loan. She knew the cost but felt she had no other choice. She had to keep the roof over her head! The consequence of her debt is that it's compounding at an astronomical rate. If she doesn't find a way to pay it off, it will swallow up all of her discretionary income. You can't sustain a 400 percent interest rate loan for long.

THE SOLUTION?

If you faced a financial setback because of COVID or other circumstances, the most important thing is to look forward, not back. Make things better for yourself, not worse. It's easier said than done if your business was shut down or your job eliminated. It's easy to feel angry, frustrated, or let anxiety and worry overrun your mind and cause you to be stuck in apathy. But that's not going to fix anything. Remember that no matter the problem, there's always a solution. At times, a financial situation can feel hopeless, but there are always steps and actions you can take to turn things around. But it has to start with you and your own initiative. Take a deep breath, and let's walk through the steps together.

Step #1: Fluff Up Your Financial Cushions

As we examined in Jenna's situation, a fully funded emergency account is more valuable than her taking a higher salary. Before you look at paying down credit cards, saving for the future, or really any other financial priority, make sure to have backup savings. Millennials and young adults fared the worst during COVID and it's not all because of their so-called avocado toast obsessions. They simply hadn't been in the labour force long enough to have savings to help them weather a financial storm as intense as COVID. Nonetheless, it should be a wake-up call to make saving priority number one moving forward.

Financial experts recommend having three to six months of your household income saved in a safe, easy-to-access bank account. That amount may seem insurmountable, especially coming off a financial crisis like COVID. However, as you learned in chapter 4 when we looked at the Thirty-Day Anti-Budget, there are ways to save without total sacrifice. Or to put this another way: once you're back on your feet and have some emergency savings built up, you can start spending on the things you miss. A little short-term pain can translate to long-term gain—and reduced stress too.

Because Jenna has a small business, she should also strive to build a corporate emergency account. Consistent cash flow is a struggle for business owners large and small. Aim to build and obtain credit even if you don't need it. Banks and lenders are in the profit game. If your situation looks risky, that's when they're least likely to provide a lifeline (or they will charge you dearly for it).

Thirty-Day Anti-Budget —COVID edition

Even though you may have spent less on plenty of goods and services during the crisis (other than groceries, the cost of which increased for 67 percent of shoppers), many of us indulged in other luxuries and guilty pleasures.[40]

According to 2018 figures from Statistics Canada, the average net savings of individuals is only $852.[41] So, if your bank account is less than that, or nonexistent, don't despair.

Where can you find some extra dough? If you factor what the average Canadian spends on eating out, alcohol, bank fees, subscriptions, and more, that adds up to about $4,750 per year. If you could cut your consumption in half, that would free up $2,375 that could fund your rainy-day account. In ten years, without factoring any interest, that would add up to a gigantic $23,750!

Paying Down Debt
Vs.
Funding Your Rainy-day Account

We have had recessions in our lifetime, but COVID was and is something else entirely. In other chapters throughout this book, I've made the case for always paying down high-interest-rate debt before accruing because with the sheer costs of servicing that debt, it just makes sense. However, when COVID hit, many families struggled to put food on the table. You never want to miss a credit card payment or ignore costly debt—but if a true emergency happens as it did for millions of Canadians with this crisis, cold, hard cash in your hands or your bank account can be life-saving.

For more ideas on building credit when you're starting out (individually or as an entrepreneur) or when you've taken a credit hit, refer back to chapter 1.

Step #2: If You Carry a Credit Card Balance, Get a Lower-rate Product

Also in chapter 1, I made the case for using your credit card to make every possible purchase to maximize your reward points. That advice absolutely does not apply if you continually carry a balance, especially if you're using a high-interest-rate credit card. Also, travel reward points aren't very enticing when you can't travel!

Jenna has a credit limit on her personal credit card of $15,000. She maxed out every month, even before COVID. She loved the reward points and racked them up. But the rewards do not outweigh the high cost of the card.

Let's look at how much her high-interest-rate card costs her:

- 19.99 percent annual rate
- 22.99 percent for cash advances
- $120 annual fee

Since she's near maxing out each month, her credit card costs her $2,995.50 each year (plus the annual fee), or $249.88 a month, not to mention the monthly $29 over-limit fee she is often charged as well.

Jenna should have called up her bank to get into a lower-rate product, but she didn't until it was too late. Most banks have credit cards that have no or exceptionally low annual fees and rates as low as 12.99 percent. While that's still a mammoth amount of interest, it's much less than the nearly 20 percent that Jenna pays.

Let's see how much Jenna would save with a lower-rate card at 12.99 percent, assuming she paid only her minimum monthly payment (3 percent of the balance each month).

Break It Down

Scenario #1: $15,000 at 19.99 percent interest:
It would take her twenty-five years to pay it off, costing her $18,340.33 in interest in addition to the $15,000. **Total cost: $33,340.33**

Scenario #2: $15,000 at 12.99 percent interest:
It would take her eighteen years to pay it off, costing her $8,309.35 in interest in addition to the $15,000. **Total cost: $23,309.35**

Savings:
That 7 percent difference from a high-interest-rate card to a no-frills card really adds up. By switching from a 19.99 percent card to a 12.99 percent card, she would have shaved seven years off her payments and saved $10,030.98 in interest. No amount of points earned could equal that. When she gets back on her feet financially, she can always opt back in to the reward card if she wants.

Unfortunately, in Jenna's situation, she was so stressed that she never looked at the rates on her credit card, nor did she crunch the numbers to see what she'd save. When she finally called up her bank for help, they wouldn't approve her request because her credit card was over the limit and she had missed a few payments.

Mental stress lowers your ability to make sound decisions and see the options available to you. When you're under constant financial pressure, it doesn't allow you to see the periphery options available.

As difficult as it can be to look at your finances, especially during times when you can't meet all of your monthly obligations, it's vitally important to do so. If you start to see your financial situation worsening, act immediately. Don't wait until you can't make a payment or you go over your credit limit. The same logic applies if you can't make a loan or mortgage payment. The same goes for utility or tax payments. Call way in advance and your lender/creditor may work with you instead of against you. Once you've missed one or more payments, they'll be far less flexible.

Pay Back with Points

Did you know that you can often use your credit card reward points to pay your credit card balance? Travel rewards will yield you the best bank for your points, but in a financial pinch, using your points can help.

Jenna had a travel points card with a large bank. It had gathered 90,000 points. She checked their redemption schedule and learned that it equaled over $500 she could use to pay down her card at least a little bit, which she did.

Step #3: Re-examine Your Housing

In the last few months, many of us have been locked down during COVID, shuttered inside our homes. And these homes are now our offices, gyms, schools, and more. A once-desirable condo in the centre of a large city may seem like a prison after months inside, especially if you have a spouse, children, or pets that you're sharing space with.

Think about how the crisis has changed how you view your home. Jenna certainly realized that her small apartment in downtown Vancouver wasn't worth the expensive monthly outlay when the crisis hit. She also realized that her friends with mortgages rather than rental payments fared much better than she did during the crisis.

How would you rate your home satisfaction level? Is it time to call up a Realtor to determine your options if you currently own? Or is it time to think about home ownership if you're renting?

Here are some considerations if you own a property:

- Condo vs. house: Would you prefer to avoid others and long waits for elevators in high-volume apartments or condos?
- Do you need a dedicated home office(s) built for you and/ or your spouse if work at home will be your reality for the coming years?
- Would a backyard have saved your family's sanity (at least for the months you can get outside in Canada)?
- If you're avoiding a long commute because you're likely to work from home in the future, would renting or buying outside of your city where the rents are far more reasonable make sense?
- Do you need to budget for renovations to make your home more conducive to working there?

Step #4: Prepare for CRA

During COVID, Jenna made a couple of dangerous missteps regarding her taxes. But she can manage this situation immediately and work with the Canada Revenue Agency to make payment arrangements to clear up her personal and GST/HST tax bill.

Many Canadians are incredibly nervous about dealing with the CRA. We've all read news reports about people losing their homes, having their bank accounts frozen, and more. The good news: like every other creditor, the CRA would prefer to work with you to design a payment arrangement rather than force collection. The bad news: the CRA can take swift and immediate legal action if you do not adhere to your arrangement. Call sooner, not later.

What Should You Expect When Speaking to a Creditor?

You should expect that you're treated fairly and with dignity. That wasn't always the case. I've heard from many Canadians over the years who have been yelled at and even harassed at work by bill collectors. This treatment is no longer acceptable, but it still happens.

When you call up your bank, CRA, or any other lender, it's best to make your call Monday to Friday, between 9 a.m. and 5 p.m., as this is when the most senior staff will be working. If you call after hours, you may reach someone with less knowledge or authority. Don't be afraid to ask for a superior to contact you. Keep careful note of the time and date of your call, whom you spoke to, and the details of the agreement.

Add any payment dates to your digital calendar and set reminders for at least a week before the payment due date.

Putting Money Away for Taxes

If you're self-employed, preparing for what's owed to CRA is always a challenge. You need to estimate what your marginal tax bracket will be (federal plus provincial taxes) for the year so you can set some money aside. You'll also want to factor in the Canada Pension Plan (CPP) dues that you'll have to pay at tax time as well.

By September 2020, Jenna earned $40,500. She made another $6,000 in the final months of the year, for a total income of $46,500. She lives in British Columbia, so her marginal tax bracket is 22.70 percent. A quick hop on the TurboTax site provides her tax-owing estimate of $10,577.

There are a number of tax credits and possible deductions (such as RRSP contributions and her self-employment expenses) that will reduce her tax burden. Make sure that you use up-to-date tax software, or a tax preparer, to ensure you're not leaving hard-earned dollars unclaimed when filing.

Step #5: Costly Protection

Balance protection on your loan or credit card can be a prudent option. But it's expensive and you want to ensure that it pays when you need it.

The cost for credit card balance protection (if you die, lose your job, or suffer a major illness) is $1.19 plus tax for every $100 on your card, calculated monthly. But check with your bank to see if their rates are different and double-check what they offer.

For Jenna, she was paying a hefty $178.50 each month and never realized it because she never checked her credit card statement. In addition to the interest she was paying on her card, it added up to over $400 a month!

Sit down with an insurance professional, especially if you're self-employed, to explore stand-alone policies in the event you suffer a disability, critical illness, or death.

Step #6: Leave RRSP Funds Be (If You Can)

RRSPs provide tax sheltering and a deduction as an incentive for Canadians to save. The more we have at retirement, the less we need to rely on the government for help like Old Age Security

(OAS) and more. However, if you take the funds out during your working lifetime, you face a quadruple whammy.

1. You don't get in your hands what you withdraw. When you take money out of your RRSP, you're subject to the following withholding tax (tax is taken off the top and sent to the government on your behalf).

Withdrawal Amount	Withholding Tax Rate (Except Quebec)	Withholding Tax Rate in Quebec
Up to $5,000	10%	5%
$5,000.01 to $15,000	20%	10%
$15,000+	30%	15%

2. You may be selling at a loss. If your investments are facing a slump, cashing them in crystalizes that loss. If your investments are down from when you bought, it's only a paper loss unless you actually sell.
3. You lose that RRSP room forever. You can't put funds back later (unless you're withdrawing for your education or buying a home for the first time).
4. Depending on your income for the year, you may have to pay even more at tax time.

We looked at what Jenna owes in taxes in Misstep #5. But that doesn't factor in her RRSP withdrawal, which she'll have to count as income. That's going to bump her into the next marginal tax bracket. Even though 20 percent of her withdrawal was held back, she'll likely have to still pay more.

Step #7: Avoid Payday Loans

It's estimated that 15 percent of renters in the month of May 2020 had to resort to expensive options like payday loans or cash advances from their credit card to make their rent payments.[42] If you have any other choice, please avoid payday lenders.

Let's look at the cost of borrowing $300 for fourteen days.[43]

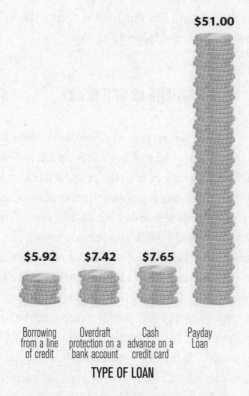

| | | | **$51.00** |

| $5.92 | $7.42 | $7.65 | |
| Borrowing from a line of credit | Overdraft protection on a bank account | Cash advance on a credit card | Payday Loan |

TYPE OF LOAN

The costs shown in this example are for illustration purposes only and are based on the following assumptions:

- A payday loan costs $17 per $100 that you borrow, which is the same as an annual interest rate of **442 percent** (that's not a typo!).
- A line of credit (not secured against your home, which would be lower) includes a $5 administration fee plus 8 percent annual interest on the amount you borrow.
- Overdraft protection on a bank account includes a $5 fee plus 21 percent annual interest on the amount you borrow.
- A cash advance on a credit card includes a $5 fee plus 23 percent annual interest on the amount you borrow.[44]

As you can see from the illustration above, the expense of a payday loan should be avoided at all costs.

WHERE IS SHE NOW?

Jenna moved in with her parents in Abbotsford. She had to lay off all but one of her staff to keep her business alive. Slowly, as the economy picked up, many of her clients came back on board with monthly retainers. The one employee she was able to keep on a reduced salary still works remotely for her. The rest of her contract staff were able to collect CERB, and Jenna's hoping she can rehire one or two of them in the near future. But for now, she's using all her income to pay her mom and dad a modest bit of rent and fast-tracking saving up for a car. She doesn't have to commute the one-hour drive to the city every day, but public transportation and walking are no longer practical from Abbotsford. Plus, since COVID, she's become a germaphobe. She's found that using a rental car once a week until she can afford to buy one is a cost-efficient alternative. Also, she's trying hard to save a bit of extra money every month for a rainy-day fund. She learned the hard way why this is so important!

Jenna's enjoying being out of the city and having a more relaxed life in Abbotsford. She's hoping to move out of her parents' house in a few months and has started looking for a roommate to share rent costs. Jenna still dreams of homeownership, but not right now, especially with experts talking about recessionary times over the coming years.

11

COVID and Your Family Finances

Juanita and Minghui are like many married couples with two younger kids. They frantically make breakfast every weekday morning, dress themselves, and then yell at their boys to hurry up for school. With both parents working full time and even overtime, they rarely spend a lot of time together as a couple until the weekend. Then the pandemic hit. Suddenly, their tiny but once comfortable house in west Toronto seemed claustrophobic.

Juanita is a prominent executive used to traveling around the country. When the COVID crisis worsened, she found herself dramatically grounded. Minghui had a contract with a small developer who was struggling before the pandemic. He gave up his low-paying contract to stay home with the boys. This meant cost savings since they no longer required a nanny.

Meanwhile, Juanita hid in their bedroom for months, conducting tiring Zoom call after Skype call. With no home office or spare rooms in the house, Juanita and Minghui's work and home situation became heated and daily arguments ensued.

Then, of course, there's Juanita's aging mother. Juanita helps her mother with many things. When her mom no longer felt safe doing banking in person, Juanita set up online banking for her. But her mother had trouble with the technology, so Juanita used her mom's password to make payments for her.

WHERE THEY WENT WRONG

Juanita and Minghui never anticipated a pandemic that would keep them homebound, but who could? Still, their finances were not on a solid trajectory before COVID and they certainly didn't improve once disaster struck.

Misstep #1: Nowhere to Work

It's not really a misstep that Juanita and Minghui never thought about creating a home office, but during the pandemic they did need a larger house than the one they had purchased. With Juanita likely not getting back to an office environment anytime soon, at least not full time, they have had to rethink their current home and work environment.

Misstep #2: Signing in to Her Mom's Bank Account

The bank lines were long during the pandemic, and Juanita's mom—like the rest of us—was told to stay home. But how was she supposed to pay her utility bills and property taxes? She is in her eighties and has a cell phone, but she just isn't tech savvy. What

Juanita didn't realize is that by using her mother's password to pay her bills for her, she was nullifying her mom's fraud protection provided by her bank.

Misstep #3: Lapsed Insurance Policy

In the flurry of the crisis, Juanita and Minghui missed three payments on their life insurance policy and it lapsed. It might not sound like a big deal, but when you miss even one life insurance policy payment (after the thirty days' grace) it nullifies the original agreement. Unlike getting your cell phone cut off and reconnecting it, life insurance contracts are based on your health at the time you apply. Juanita has had some health issues since they first took out their policy years ago. Because it lapsed, the new premiums shot right up.

Misstep #4: Missed Payments

During the lockdown, Minghui paid his cell phone bill late. He also missed a couple of payments on his credit cards. He didn't think it was a big deal. But he didn't realize how much it would affect his credit score, dropping it down from an excellent rating of 840 to a good rating of 743.

Misstep #5: Double Paying for Benefits

With a terribly busy household before COVID, Juanita and Minghui never examined their benefits plans. Because Minghui was a contract worker, he purchased his own private health care policy years ago . . . which was smart, except that Juanita's work plan covers a number of benefits for him already. The extra plan is wasted money that could go toward debt repayment.

Misstep #6: Mortgage Deferral Holiday

As of June 2020, Canadian banks had processed over 450,000 credit card deferral requests and over 740,000 mortgage deferral requests. The top six banks have deferred mortgage repayments at nearly double the rate of their US counterparts, accounting for approximately 16 percent of their mortgage portfolios, which amounts to over $250 billion. The president of the Canada Mortgage and Housing Corporation (CMHC) has expressed his concerns with the deferral situation, including the prospect of up to 20 percent of Canadian mortgages falling into arrears.[45]

When the pandemic hit, financial experts suggested that consumers take advantage of the offer to defer mortgage payments. Many people used this offer to top up their emergency savings with the money they would normally have put toward their mortgage. Juanita and Minghui took the six-month mortgage deferral offer from their bank, but they failed to actually create an emergency fund with these savings. Instead, they buried the money in their backyard. They bought lawn furniture, a barbeque, and expensive toys—and a pool—to keep the boys busy outside during the summer. Who can blame them? They were desperate to keep their children entertained at home. But the deferral holiday lasted only so long and is soon about to come to a screeching halt.

Misstep #7: Sold Low

During the spring of 2020, it was hard not to panic about investments. Every day, news anchors reported record lows in the stock market. Forget the massive decline of the 2008/2009 financial crisis—the COVID-19 world shutdown was far worse than the Great Depression, so we were told.

It's no wonder Juanita and Minghui were worrying about their investments, even though it would be a decade and a half before they retired. In early April 2020, they turned all of their equity investments into cash, hoping they could lessen the damage already done to their portfolios. Many of their friends were doing the same thing. Following what your friends do with their investments is akin to taking medication that their doctors prescribed for your own health issues. If you're selling your investments during a time of uncertainty, contact a professional. Don't act on the advice of those in your social circle.

THE SOLUTION?

There is a simple, ten-step method for getting your finances back on track if they've been derailed during the pandemic. Simple doesn't mean easy, though. It's time for Juanita and Minghui to create a healthy relationship with money going forward. And to start to heal from the financial blow of COVID.

Step #1: Take Advantage of Deferrals if You Must

Hopefully, we will never again see a financial catastrophe like we have with COVID-19. But when you face financial hardship, you may have no option but to ask for deferrals or payment arrangements from your creditors. It's vitally important that you keep track of the details, new due dates, and restrictions.

Make a list of the following deferrals:

- Mortgage
- Credit card
- Utility

- Property tax
- GST/HST
- Income tax

Keep track of due dates, amounts owed, interest rates, and deferral regulations. See which deferrals you can negotiate vis-à-vis reduced interest rates or costs. Add all your bills and due dates to your online/digital calendar. Add reminders two weeks in advance of deferral deadlines.

Did you know that you can add alerts to your credit cards and bank accounts too? Each time a transaction is made (a purchase, withdrawal, bill payment), you receive a text or email. This is also a great way to keep an eye out—in real time—for possible fraudulent activity on your accounts.

Step #2: Know Your Credit Score

Missing even one payment can affect your credit score. But missing a few can pull it down significantly. Don't stress if yours took a hit during the pandemic. With consistent habits and some time, you can get your score back up.

If you're applying for a car loan, line of credit, mortgage, or even asking for an increase on your credit card, you may be denied because of a poor score. And not all lenders view your score consistently. Some may think 743 is a very good score, whereas others view that as just passable.

Juanita and Minghui could have used a line of credit to help them feel more secure during the pandemic. As their mortgage deferrals ran out, a line of credit could have provided them a buffer to dip into if they still needed some cash flow. But because they contacted their bank when Minghui's score had already suffered a hit, they were declined. When they go to renew their car and auto insurance in a few months, their premiums may increase as a result.

During COVID, both Equifax and TransUnion were offering free credit reports online. You could check as often as you liked at no cost. Ideally, when you make a deferral, you want to review your report in thirty days to see that it has not been registered by your creditor as a default, which would hurt your score. And by the way, I'm often asked by readers if checking hurts their score. Don't worry: it doesn't.

You can use a free credit score service, but make sure you read the fine print and are comfortable with that company having your personal information. Be sure to check on your bank or credit card app as well. They may offer you the ability to check your score for free.

If your credit score was impacted because of a job loss, health issue, or other issue, you can now add a Consumer Statement with both Equifax and TransUnion. This is a short sentence that lets lenders know what happened. For example: "I lost my job due to COVID-19 and fell behind on some debts. I'm now working and anticipate all accounts to be in good standing moving forward."

Let's look at Minghui's credit score.

He has two credit cards with different banks. When he reviews his online banking, he sees that both banks offer free credit scores. He checks with the first and is pleasantly surprised that his score of 743 is rated as "very good." When he checks with the second, he's disappointed that they rated the same 743 score as "good."

Different lenders interpret your score in different ways. It's helpful to note that Minghui's score isn't any better at 788 than it is at 743. Why? It's the bands that the lender cares about. So, until his score is 790 or above, he wouldn't be in the "very good" band with a big bank.

Now, if Minghui isn't applying for any new credit, his score isn't really affecting his life. However, if his score drags down consistently and he falls into the "fair" or "poor" band, it is possible for his credit card issuer to peek into his credit report and reduce his available credit or even demand he pays off his credit card in full. This doesn't happen often in Canada (more so during financial crises in the US), but it does happen. It's important to know that a credit card is a demand loan. And yes, that means your lender can demand payment at any time for any reason, unlike a mortgage or loan that has specific terms of payment. And how did they peek into your credit report? In the fine print of the terms and conditions of your credit card agreement, it's a stipulation that at any time, the lender can check up on your debt payments, history, and score.

Step #3: Understand Your Benefits and Monitor Your Investments

Juanita and Minghui were double-paying on their work benefits. If you and your spouse are lucky enough to have medical and health benefits covered by an employer, ask yourself: Are you and your spouse able to reap similar benefits from just one plan rather than buying a second one? If so, time to cancel the plan you're paying for out of pocket.

Many people had to put investments on hold during the crisis. But you can't forget entirely about them. Ask yourself:

- Did you stop RRSP, TFSA, or group RRSP payments? If so, when can you start them again? Can you start them soon at a reduced rate, just to get back into the habit of saving?

- If you made RRSP contributions but suffered an income loss, can you defer your tax deduction to a more advantageous year in the future when your income increases? (Remember: the size of your tax deduction from an RRSP is directly determined by your marginal tax bracket—the higher it is, the higher the deduction.)
- Can you defer your tax refund to a more advantageous year if you or your spouse experienced reduced income? For example, if your income dropped this year or is low and you expect it will be higher in, say, three years, you can still make your RRSP contribution this year and use your tax deduction in the year that your income is higher. This generates a higher deduction.

Juanita and Minghui both stopped their automatic RRSP and TFSA monthly savings during the pandemic. But when their economic situation improved, they didn't resume the payments.

If you stopped investment contributions, see if you can resume them, even at a fraction of what you invested previously, just to get back in the habit. Then, put a reminder in your calendar for every two months to see if you can increase the amounts saved. (Even a dollar a day more can really add up over time.)

Step #4: Go Back to Your Old Savings Habits As Soon As You Can

Many Canadians found a silver lining to the slow pace of life during COVID: extra money in their account. If you found yourself saving quite a bit of money amid the shutdown, put that money to work right away.

When is the best time to invest? The reality is no one ever knows. So, how do you get into the stock market strategically?

The best way is to buy on the same day every month, over several months or a year, rather than invest a large amount on any single, particular day. The idea is to take advantage of monthly stock market ups and downs by taking the guesswork out of it. Buy on a certain day of the month regardless of where the market is at (or, if you're selling, do so over several months on a certain day).

Let's look at an example using the S&P 500 Index over a one-year period from September 26, 2019, to September 25, 2020.

The high for the index was 3,580.84 on September 2, 2020, and the low was 2,237.40 on March 23, 2020. If you'd like to see a graph of this, simply google S&P 500 and you can look at the index over a day, week, month, year, or five years.

If you were a stock market wizard, you would have bought on March 23, but no one knew that was the low.

Given the dollar-cost averaging advice above, let's look at how your money would have fared if you invested on the fifteenth of each month (for months where the fifteenth falls on a weekend, you'd be investing on the following business day):

October 15, 2019:	Index closed at 2,995.68
November 15, 2019:	Index closed at 3,120.46
December 16, 2019:	Index closed at 3,191.45
January 15, 2020:	Index closed at 3,289.29
February 17, 2020:	Index closed at 3,370.29
March 16, 2020:	Index closed at 2,386.13
April 15, 2020:	Index closed at 2,783.36
May 15, 2020:	Index closed at 2,863.70
June 16, 2020:	Index closed at 3,066.59
July 15, 2020:	Index closed at 3,226.56
August 17, 2020:	Index closed at 3,381.99
September 15, 2020:	Index closed at 3,401.20

That gives you an average buy price from October 15, 2019, to September 15, 2020, of 3089.73—certainly not the low of 2237.40 but far less than the high of 3580.84 for the year. You can see how buying at regular intervals each month smooths out the ups and downs and gives you a reasonable average over a year or more.

At the height of the stock market woes, investors were panicking and agitated. My email was blowing up with reporters and producers wanting opinions on whether people should sit tight with their investments or sell.

When a *Toronto Star* article titled "Close to Retirement? Don't Panic, Says Financial Experts" came out on March 22, 2020, containing my advice for investors to stay the course, I have to say it even made me a little queasy as the stock market continued to plummet for weeks.

But I've been through the stock market downturn of 1994, the tech bust of 2000, and the financial crisis of 2008/2009. During the latter crash, I remember CNBC and BNN news anchors nervously reporting that it was "worse than the Great Depression." We heard the media use a great deal of the same language during the pandemic of 2020. I always encourage people to avoid acting out of fear.

Let me put this another way. When we are stressed, we feel that doing something is better than nothing. You want your advisor to buy or sell or do something to ease your uncertainty and panic. Avoid this route. Why? Because investments are like a bar of soap. The more you touch them, the smaller they get.

Step #5: Know the Real Cost of Mortgage Deferrals

If you deferred your mortgage, let's dig into the impact and benefits. Let's take an example of a $200,000 mortgage balance at a 3.00 percent fixed interest rate with a six-month deferral and a remaining amortization of fifteen years.

The deferral would free up $8,274 of cash for you (six payments of $1,379 each) over that period.

In this example, during the deferral period, interest continues to accrue and is added to the mortgage balance at the end of the deferral period. With this case, $3,018 in interest is added to the mortgage balance. At the end of the deferral period, the payments stay the same, but the remaining amortization is extended by six months. Keep in mind that some lenders increased customers' monthly payments at the end of the deferral period (instead of increasing their amortization).

Juanita and Minghui were relieved that their bank didn't increase their monthly payment at the end of their deferral. Their mortgage amortization increased by a year and two months. But when they're back on their financial footing, they can always get back to where they were by making lump-sum payments to their mortgage.

Step #6: Know What's Tax Deductible and What's Not

Juanita found that she simply couldn't keep working from her tiny bedroom. After setting up the backyard of their dreams, replete with a state-of-the-art barbeque/outdoor kitchen and a top-of-the-line trampoline for the kids, the couple had used up $3,200 of the mortgage deferral. Juanita and Minghui spent the rest of their mortgage deferral money on finishing a small room in the basement, which became her home office. That expense set her back around $5,074.

Juanita and Minghui incurred costs for office supplies or furnishings big and small, and are wondering what they can claim on their taxes and what they can't. It all depends on the type of work you do, so let's break down the three main types of employment most people face:

Self-employed

COVID hasn't changed much for this class of employment. If you've always had a home office, you've likely used parts of your home and other expenses (cell phone, internet, etc.) to offset your income. If you've made large purchases, such as a car or renovations to your home office, these would be considered Capital Cost Allowances (CCA), meaning that you are able to deduct an amount each year of the depreciation (not the entire cost). If Minghui was still working as an independent contractor and seeing clients at their home, he would likely have been able to deduct a portion of his family's mortgage interest costs, utilities, and even the bottled water they had delivered against his earnings.

Employed and Paid Salary and Commissions

This class of employee may claim some expenses depending on how they relate specifically to their job. If this is you, fill out a T2200, which is a Declaration of Conditions of Employment form that allows certain employees to deduct specific expenses that are incurred for the purpose of earning employment income. These expenses may include your car, home office, or travel expenses. You'll have to prove that these costs were essential to the performance of your job, and your employer will have to fill out the form with you. While this option has always applied to this type of commissioned employee, COVID might have forced you to incur more expenses than ever before.

Juanita is paid a salary plus commissions in her executive role. Because she used to work at her employer's office tower but is now at home for the foreseeable future, her expenses on her T2200 skyrocketed. She had clients over to her home in lieu of entertaining out, not to mention all of the bottled water and increase to her water and power bills. She'll need to ensure that she keeps up to date with CRA's guidance on deductible expenses related to COVID.

Employed

If you're traditionally employed (and don't earn commissions) and need to incur costs to do your job at home, your best option is to have your employer reimburse your costs and have them expense the deduction.

Regardless of how you're paid, if you were conducting 50 percent or more of your work from home during the pandemic, you may be able to claim some expenses such as rent, maintenance, and utilities. You'll have to prove to CRA that you used home space to earn employment income and that it was necessary for your employment duties.

At the time of writing this book, CRA still had not provided clear guidance to Canadians working from home and the specific expenses that can be deducted. Please visit kelleykeehn.com/talk-moneytome for the CRA's current guidance on this issue.

If you faced extensive expenses because of the pandemic, it may make sense to seek the counsel of a Chartered Professional Accountant (CPA) to ensure that you're taking advantage of every possible tax benefit and expense.

Step #7: Deferring the Tax Deduction on Your RRSP Contributions When Income Drops

As you learned in chapter 3, the larger your marginal tax bracket, the greater your tax deduction when investing in an RRSP. This is a big perk, in addition to the tax sheltering until you take the money out.

Minghui's income dropped to zero in 2020 and 2021 when he opted to stay home with the kids during COVID. Because Juanita and Minghui's mortgage payment didn't increase after their deferrals, they restarted both of their RRSP contributions in January 2021. Minghui doesn't have any income but anticipates getting back to work in 2022. His advisor suggested he keep investing but use the tax deduction in a later year when his income increases. He can defer that deduction indefinitely.

Step #8: Consider a Spousal RRSP if One Spouse's Income Has Changed

A spousal RRSP is designed to smooth out income for a couple at retirement. Let's assume Minghui stays home with the kids for several years and Juanita makes the bulk or all of the income for the household. She also has a pension, so that would mean she'll be drawing more out of her pension and investments than Minghui at retirement, putting her in a higher tax bracket. Wouldn't it be great if she could split some of the income with Minghui and reduce her tax payable? In fact, they can set that arrangement up now. It's too late if they wait until retirement.

A spousal RRSP allows the higher-income-earning spouse (or the spouse that is estimated to have more income at retirement) to invest in the other spouse's name.

Step #9: Act Quickly if You've Missed a Life Insurance Policy Payment

Most insurance policies have a thirty-day grace period for you to make up your payment before the insurance coverage is terminated. If you go past that time period, the policy lapses.

You can bring your policy back to life by reinstating it. You'll need to pay the outstanding premiums and go through possible new underwriting. This may mean an increase in premiums.

Juanita and Minghui met with their insurance agent. Because they were over four months behind on making their payments, they couldn't reinstate their policy at their old rate. They were shocked to hear their premiums would increase by nearly 40 percent. Juanita has a sizeable death coverage with her work benefit plan, so she and Minghui decided to limit the amount of coverage with this new policy to stay at around the same monthly payment as before. However, they should keep in mind that if Juanita quits her job or is fired, she'll lose that benefit of employment.

Step #10: Don't Risk Someone's Fraud Protection

Juanita put her mom at risk by logging in to her account. If her mom had been the victim of fraud, she would not have been covered for any losses.

Instead of putting her mom at risk, Juanita could have invested more time in teaching her mom how to use the bank app. If that wasn't viable, she could have talked to her mother about making her power of attorney. This would make it legal for Juanita to do her mom's banking and use her credit card without violating her fraud protection. She could also get a supplementary card on her mom's account so she could make purchases with the account with her very own card.

WHERE ARE THEY NOW?

Following months of nagging financial fears and sleepless nights, Juanita and Minghui booked three financial date nights in the calendar over a span of six weeks. Knowing they would be talking about money on these predetermined days allowed them to pre-pare in advance. After each get-together, they were slowly gaining more control of their finances and feeling more like a united team.

And after their third date night, they realized they needed pro-fessional financial help. They had a few conversations with their banker over Zoom. They learned they could pay an extra $200 a month on their mortgage, and in five years, this would reverse the deferrals they obtained during COVID. They also had a virtual call with a nonprofit credit counselor to walk Minghui through some tips for getting his credit score back up and keeping it high. The best advice was for him to set up automatic payments with his cell phone provider so he'd never miss a payment. All of this con-certed effort has brought this couple closer together—and not just financially!

Where Are You Now?

You made it to the end! You've seen the mistakes we all make with our money, and hopefully you've learned something along the way. If nothing else, I hope you've learned that there is almost always a solution to the problem, and you don't have to fix it by yourself. There are resources and professionals aplenty to help get you back on track with your finances. If you're facing a financial misstep, chances are high that someone else has also already faced the same problem—and survived it.

As we near the end of this portion of your journey to greater financial literacy and well-being, I wish you success and prosperity, and I want to remind you to have fun with it. There is power and joy that comes from financial independence and knowledge. Enjoy it!

I'll leave you with just a few parting words, and ask that you remember two things. First, remember that when you make one change, no matter how small, you are changing the whole system. Take the chemical compounds in a glass of water, for example: if you add just one drop of lemon juice, it's no longer H_2O—it's something else entirely. The same goes for the changes you'll make to your daily life after reading this book. If you take just one drop of advice from this book and apply it to your life, you'll change your entire financial system. Pretty exciting, right?

When you change your life, you also change the lives of those around you. By taking action toward change (whether it's a big or small step), you can positively influence the financial lives of your friends, family, coworkers, and loved ones. This is true for people both far and near. How powerful does that feel? Keep that in mind as you check your own credit, open up an investment account, or simply take the time to organize your bills. By doing so, you create a space for your new financially empowered life.

Second, I ask that you remember that feeling good about money takes practice. Consider that getting financially healthy is a bit like a yoga or meditation practice—it will take work and consistency. As with any other worthwhile pursuit, financial well-being won't happen overnight. I like to say that what you appreciate, appreciates! Even if you focus just a little bit of your time to consistently improving your money matters, you'll see a positive change.

Now I leave you to ably conquer your world—one money milestone at a time. And I'm not really gone for good. I'd love to hear from you! If you have a question, need a pat on the back, or if you're looking to expand your reading and literary education, I'm happy to help. What worked for you? What improvements did you make? And finally, did you start talking about money?! I hope you've opened up the conversation with your friends and loved ones with the goal of helping everyone to feel good about money.

Kelley Keehn

Glossary

amortization: This is how long you have to pay off your mortgage. Think of it as the gradual time it takes to pay back a big debt. In Canada, you can have an amortization of up to twenty-five years.

asset: An investment that you own in your name and hope will increase in value over time, such as a house, piece of art, or a collector car.

beneficiary: The person whom you name to inherit your money or other benefits when you pass away.

bond: As an investor, when you own a bond, you're *owed* money. The interest is fixed and is considered income that you're paid annually or more frequently, which is why this asset class is often referred to as a *fixed income*.

cash: A cash asset is an investment that is easily accessible but for which you get a meager return in interest because current interest rates are very low.

Certified Financial Planner: A professional in the personal finance industry certified with the most widely recognized financial planning designation in Canada. They provide financial planning strategies and solutions and work with you to create a financial plan that works for you—no matter how big or small the problem.

collections account: If you have something "in collections," a debt is outstanding and grossly overdue—it usually takes ninety days or more for your lender to write off a debt and send it to a collection agency to try to recoup the funds.

credit score: Your credit score can range from 300 to 900. While high scores are the most favourable, only an estimated 5 percent of Canadians have a score over 850, and it's the range that matters, not the actual number. A credit report will indicate where your score stands in the following ranges: Poor, Fair, Good, Very Good, or Excellent.

defined benefit plan: A pension plan in which your company guarantees your retirement payment lump sum amount that you'll receive at retirement. These plans are almost as rare today as a unicorn.

defined contribution plan: A pension plan in which you know what you and your employer are contributing, but there is no set amount you'll have at retirement.

demand loan: A form of loan where the creditor can demand that you pay your balance in full immediately, and it can be called in at any time. These loans are usually made on credit cards, a line of credit, or some student loans, and the demand for payment often comes as a result of a creditor checking your credit report and noticing that you've missed or have been behind in payments. It is rare that a loan is called in, but it does happen!

dividend: A financial bonus for investing in a company (when you buy a preferred share).

emergency fund: A fully funded emergency account, which should contain three to six months of your household income. If you're self-employed, have a highly specialized job, or work in an unstable industry, an emergency fund should cover as much as one year of your household income.

gross income: Total income before the deduction of any fees. Most commonly, gross income refers to income before tax deductions.

Group Registered Retirement Savings Plan (Group RRSP): A savings plan to which you contribute payments from each paycheque, and it is administered by your employer. These are the most popular with employers today.

hard credit inquiry: These inquiries result from actively seeking credit and can affect your credit score. If you apply for a new car loan, credit card, or even cell phone, you agree to have a credit check performed, which will appear on your credit score as a hard inquiry.

Home Buyers' Plan: This is a provision that allows you to take money out of your RRSP without paying tax if you're a first-time home buyer. You can withdraw up to $25,000 from your plan in a calendar year. You have to start making payments back to your RRSP in the second year and generally have fifteen years to pay yourself back, but you can do so at any time. You will be taxed on your withdrawal if you don't comply with the Government of Canada's rules.

line of credit: A line of credit is like a credit card with no card attached to it and offers a much better interest rate, and it doesn't cost you anything unless you use it.

liquidity: Your investments are liquid when you can sell the assets quickly and get your money back when you need it. A house, real estate, and art are all examples of investments that aren't very liquid because they take time to sell.

mortgage: A long-term loan against your house provided by a bank or other lender. A mortgage requires you to make payments over a longer period, between ten and twenty-five years.

mutual fund: A pool of investments that includes the professional services of a mutual fund manager. There are thousands of mutual funds available in the Canadian marketplace, which range in level of risk and return opportunities.

net income: Total income after taxes are deducted. It's what you have left in your bank before paying any expenses.

net worth statement: A calculation that balances out how much you own and how much you owe to give you a full picture of your financial health. The exercise of calculating your net worth encourages you to dig through your assets and debts.

nonprofit credit counsellor: A professional in the personal finance industry who can offer an initial financial assessment at no cost to you, and can provide options for getting out of debt after reviewing your income, expenses, assets, and debts.

power of attorney (POA): Someone that can act on your behalf while you're alive. The minute you pass away, their power ceases, and your executor steps in to help handle your estate. They can be the same person, but they don't have to be.

Registered Education Savings Plan (RESP): A registered savings plan that you set up to save for your child's education. There are no tax deductions, and there is a lifetime contribution limit of $50,000 per child in your household.

Registered Retirement Income Fund (RRIF): An income fund that results from converting your RRSPs by the end of the year that you turn seventy-one. This requires a simple change form and converts all of the assets you had in your RRSP (stocks, bonds, mutual funds, GICs, etc.) into a new plan that provides a source of income. All of your investments will continue to grow tax deferred, but you can't add any new funds and you must take out a minimum payment from your plan each year.

Registered Retirement Savings Plan (RRSP): A retirement savings plan that you establish and contribute to, and the money in the plan grows tax deferred—you won't pay any tax until you start withdrawing money, which usually happens at retirement.

secured card: A secured card is a credit card that requires you to deposit money with the bank as a form of security in case you are unable to make payments. If you want to get a credit limit of $300, you would provide $300 in the bank in advance. It's a good way to establish credit.

soft credit inquiry: These credit inquiries do not count against your score but will still appear on your report. These result from you or a company checking your credit as part of a background check. You can check your credit report as often as you like without it affecting your score.

stock: You can purchase shares—or equity—to have partial ownership in a company in the form of stock. If the company does well, you do well, but if the company tanks or goes bankrupt, you could lose everything.

tax-free savings account (TFSA): When you have money in a TFSA, your money is truly tax free: it can grow and be withdrawn tax free. A TFSA, like an RRSP or an RESP, is the garage shielding your car from taxation, and can contain multiple investments.

Acknowledgments

Although I've never purchased a lottery ticket for myself, I won the parent jackpot with my mom and hero, Kathleen Keehn. No project in my life ever starts or ends without her undying love and enthusiasm. To echo the words of Abraham Lincoln, "All that I am or ever hope to be, I owe to my mother."

No book in my life would have ever been written without the encouragement of my husband, Wyatt Cavanaugh. He first planted the seeds in my doubting mind fourteen years ago, and it's only with his vision and love that this undertaking was even a possibility.

To Rachel Wood for bringing her husband to our cocktail meeting in Vancouver so many years ago. And to Brian Wood, who became my literary agent over a strong scotch that afternoon. I didn't think I had another book in me, but you knew otherwise. If it wasn't for your belief in my mission for Canadians to feel good about money and your expertise, this book would have never been born.

Acknowledgments

To Nita Pronovost at Simon and Schuster—you showed me such grace and kindness when you said "no, but" to my first book proposal. And for saying, "yes, and" to the second one. This book is as much your creation as mine, and I thank you for your brilliant oversight on this project. To Siobhan Doody, my wonderful editor, for your savvy skills and excitement during every step of the publication of this book. You allowed me to have the confidence to just write, knowing your red pen would make the content palatable and even pop for our readers. And to Kevin Hanson, head of Simon and Schuster. As a businesswoman and an author who self-published her first book, I know how incredibly lucky I am to have had this title chosen as one of your publications. Thank you also to Felicia Quon, Jessica Rattray, and Rebecca Snoddon for your help getting the book into readers' hands. It's an author's dream to work with such a dynamic and professional team of passionate fellow literature lovers.

To my mentors Marilyn Denis and David Chilton. Your friendship and guidance over the years has been incredibly valuable to me and has benefited this book immensely.

To Cary List and the amazingly dedicated team at FP Canada. It's been an honour to be your consumer advocate. Your research and tireless efforts to empower and educate Canadians on all matters of financial planning has and will continue to contribute to the financial well-being of this wonderful country. Shout-outs to Ralph Vizl, Nicholas Cheung, Megan Harman, Liz Ptak, Stephen Rotstein, Joan Yudelson (FP Canada Research Foundation), Damienne Lebrun-Reid, Joanna Tukums, Joan Vanden Hazel, Daniel Ongara, Manos Geramas, Tomo Hayashi, and to past and present board members Tina Di Vito, Dan Busi, Brett Millard, Caroline Dabu, Dawn Hawley, Martin Dupras, François Durocher, Carolyn Fallis, Yves Giroux, Ronald Harvey, Pat Macdonald, Peter Shen, and David Wild.

To Commissioner Lucie Tedesco, Financial Literacy Leader Jane Rooney, and your phenomenal team at the Financial Consumer Agency of Canada. It's been a great privilege to have worked with you both over the years as you and your team have created greater awareness and practical tools to support the financial literacy and well-being of all Canadians. Special thanks to Julie Hauser, Andre-Marc Allain, Pierre Bisson, Elizabeth LaForest, Bruno Levesque, Emilie Rene, Maria Vranas, Jeremy Ryan, Steve Trites, Lynn Santerre, Marilyn Leblanc, Maryam Farhat, Mehdi Jeeroburkhan, Michael Olson, RuthAnne Corley, and Dr. Rebecca Kong.

To the many champions of financial literacy in this country who have also greatly benefited this project: Allison Riva and Gary Rabbior from the Canadian Foundation for Economic Education; Dr. Dilip Soman and the phenomenal team the Behavioural Economics in Action Research Centre at Rotman (BEAR); Fabio Bonano from CPA Canada and Lucy Becker from IIROC; Laurie Campbell, Adriana Molina and Keith Emery from Credit Canada; Tyler Fleming and your incredible team at the Ontario Securities Commission; Alison Trollope and your team at the Alberta Securities Commission; Rick Hancox, Peter Klohn, Andrew Nicholson, Sara Wilson, and Erin King from FCNB (Financial and Consumer Services Commission); Darin Diehl, Nicole Francis, and Mark Nicholson from Tangerine; Julie Kuzmic from Equifax; Liz Mulholland from Prosper Canada; Rob Carrick from the *Globe and Mail*; Tom Reid and John Haliburton from Sun Life Financial; Duane Green from Franklin Templeton Mutual Funds; Caroline Dabu from the Bank of Montreal; Jacqueline O'Flanagan, Sol Amos; Dr. Tom Keenan; Jennifer Fiddian-Green; Preet Banerjee; Melissa Leong; Bruce Sellery; Aaron Broverman; Russell and Christine Cullingworth; Graham Neil; Barry Choi, Kristine Leadbetter; Robert Hoshowsky; Robin Taub; Greg Bonnell from BNN Bloomberg; Larysa Harapyn from Postmedia; Tracey Bissett,

Acknowledgments

Jordan Wilson; Maili Wong; Lana Sanichar from *Canadian MoneySaver* magazine; Michael Lee Chin from Portland Holdings Limited; Diana Oddi from Mandeville Private Client Inc.; Mike O'Connor; Gillian Buckley; Dan Varrette; Dr. Moira Somers; Jason Heath from Objective Financial Partners Inc.; Shawn Todd from Ecivda; John DeGoey from Wellington-Altus Private Wealth; Larry Berman and Jared Rabinowitz from ETF Capital Management; Shawn Graham; Corey Baker; Jim Thorne and the entire staff and board at Money Mentors; Sheila Walkington from Money Coaches Canada; Shannon Lee Simmons from the New School of Finance; Aashti Vijh, Matt Hands, and Tara Bloger from Ratehub.ca; Greg Mackling, Brett Megarry, and Lauren McNabb from CJOB radio; Nicole Dube and the CTV Winnipeg team; J'lyn Ney and Ryan Jespersen from 630 CHED radio; Daryl McIntyre, Stacey Brotzel, Rob Williams, Graham Neil, Nahreman Issa, Cory Edel, Kevin Youngblut, and the CTV Edmonton team; Andrew Carter and Sarah Deshaies from CJAD; Jennifer Crosby, Shaye Ganam, Mike Sobel, and the Global News Edmonton team; Dalls Flexhaug, Leslie Horton, Joel Senick, Tracy Nagai, and the Global News Calgary team; Leslie Goldstone, Rod Kurtz, Adrienne Pan, Peter Brown (formerly), Mark Schultz (formerly), and my CBC Radioactive family; Barb DiGiulio and Ben Harrison from Newstalk 1010 Toronto; Jefferson Humphreys and the entire CTV Calgary team; Peter Watts, Gord Gilles, Sue Deyell, and the entire team at Global News Radio 770 in Calgary; Dahlia Kurtz from CFRA radio; Annette Goerner, Trish Owens, and the team at CTV Ottawa; Joanne Richards from Postmedia; Sharon Henderson, Janine Reed, and Kate Funston from Chartwell Retirement Residences; Elizabeth Naumovski, Judy Paradi, and Paulette Filion from Strategy Marketing; Ellen Roseman from the *Toronto Star*; Lana Sanichar, Shelley Clayton, Doretta Thompson, Tashia Batstone, Li Zhang, and Odette Lawrence from CPA Canada.

To the gifted team that managed my business and media life during this project. Miroki Tong, my general manager; Terance Brouse, Emma Niham, Jessica Patriquin, and Lyndsay Wallis from Maverick PR; and Jaimy Warner and her team at the Social Smiths; and my website wiz, Renae Quinton, and Electric Villages. To my work family—I love you all dearly.

To my loving family for your patience and acceptance of my many missed family appearances. I thank you for your understanding, passion for my work, and much needed love and support. My brothers Randy and David; my sister-in-law, Elaine; and my nieces and nephew, Amelia, Dr. Alysha Keehn, Jay, and Adam. To my dear friends Carl Sawyer, Bill Rosser, Jennifer Chan, my spice girl Lisa McMyn, Lynn Johnston, Drew Williston, Gregory Schiltroth, Jackie Foord, Alyson and Mark Connolly, Heather and Sue Secord, Dr. Amy D'Aprix, Mary Atkin, and the wonderful women at Verity. To my gifted style team: Voula Zi, Aaron O'Bryan, Luis Zulayhka, and Katie Tobin. And my heart-focused business coach, Dr. Friedemann Schaub, and coaches Hina Khan, Kelly Swartz, Jocelyn Hill, and Mark Bowden. And to my good friend and colleague Kimberley Ney for encouraging me to write this book years ago.

Last but never least, to my cats, Niles and Fraser, for your welcomed interruptions during my writing process. Your unconditional love and playtime made completing this more fun. And to my creator for giving me the life force to tackle another book.

Notes

Introduction

1   Priyanka Correia, "COVID-19 Study: Vulnerable Canadians Falling Through the Cracks," Loans Canada, accessed September 28, 2020, https://loanscanada.ca/stats/covid-19-study-vulnerable-canadians-falling-through-the-cracks.

1. Cash or Credit?

2   Alyssa Furtado, "How Much Do I Have to Spend on a Credit Card to Breakeven?" Ratehub.ca, March 23, 2015, https://www.ratehub.ca/blog/how-much-do-i-have-to-spend-on-a-credit-card-to-breakeven/.

3   Andrew Russell and David Akin, "Stats Canada Requesting Banking Information of 500,000 Canadians without Their Knowledge," *Global News*, October 26, 2018, https://globalnews.ca/news/4599953/exclusive-stats-canada-requesting-banking-information-of-500000-canadians-without-their-knowledge/.

4   FP Canada, "Why Canadians Worry About Money," Financial

Planning for Canadians, accessed July 29, 2019, https://www
.financialplanningforcanadians.ca/financial-planning/canadians
-worry-about-money.

5   Aaron Broverman, "Canadian Credit Card, Debit Card and
Debt Statistics," Creditcards.com, January 4, 2018, https://www
.creditcards.com/credit-card-news/canada-credit-card-debit
-card-stats-international-1276.php.

2. Shopaholic Anonymous

6   "Canadian Household Debt Hits $1.8 Trillion as Global Watch-
dog Warns of Risks to Economy," *Financial Post*, March 12,
2018, https://business.financialpost.com/personal-finance/debt
/canadian-household-debt-hits-1-8t-as-report-warns-of-do
mestic-risk.

7   See note 5.

8   FP Canada, "Money and Mental Health," Financial Planning
for Canadians, accessed July 29, 2019, https://www.finan
cialplanningforcanadians.ca/financial-planning/money
-and-mental-health-survey?rq=money%20and%20mental%20
health.

3. Leaving Money on the Table

9   Rob Carrick, "Canadians Are Passing Up Billions of Dollars in
Pension Plan Contributions from Their Employers," *Globe and
Mail*, June 25, 2019, https://www.theglobeandmail.com/investing
/personal-finance/article-canadians-are-passing-up-billions-of
-dollars-in-pension-plan/.

10   Linda Babcock and Sara Laschever, "Introduction," in *Women
Don't Ask: Negotiation and the Gender Divide* (Princeton:
Princeton University Press, 2003), 5.

11   Maureen McCarty, "Salary Stats: Women vs. Men," Washington
Post.com, November 7, 2008, http://www.washingtonpost.com
/wp-dyn/content/article/2008/11/06/AR2008110602982.html
?noredirect=on.

4. All Show

12 Deborah Baic, "The True Cost of Keeping Up with the Joneses," *The Globe and Mail*, April 8, 2016, https://www.theglobe andmail.com/report-on-business/careers/business-educa tion/the-true-cost-of-keeping-up-with-the-joneses/article 29491497/.

13 Shaurya Malway, "Twenty-One Percent of College Students Use Their Loans to Invest in Cryptocurrencies," *Inside Bitcoins*, March 24, 2018, https://insidebitcoins.com/news/21-percent-of -college-students-use-their-loans-to-invest-in-cryptocurrencies /116682.

5. The Car Trap

14 Ben Bryant, "Judges Are More Lenient after Taking a Break, Study Finds," *The Guardian*, April 11, 2011, https://www.theguardian .com/law/2011/apr/11/judges-lenient-break.

15 FP Canada, "Money and Mental Health: Canadians More Embarrassed about Their Financial Situation Than Four Years Ago," newswire.ca, May 7, 2018, https://www.newswire.ca/news -releases/money-and-mental-health-canadians-more-embarrassed -about-their-financial-situation-than-four-years-ago-681930421 .html.

6. Sharing Is Caring

16 FP Canada, "Women and Financial Independence," Financial Planning for Canadians, accessed July 29, 2019, https://www .financialplanningforcanadians.ca/financial-planning/financial -independence-survey.

17 FP Canada, "Financial Infidelity: What's Love Got to Do With Money?," Financial Planning for Canadians, accessed July 29, 2019, https://www.financialplanningforcanadians.ca/financial-planning /financial-infidelity.

18 Ben Steverman, "Do You Know What Your Spouse Makes? 43

Percent of Americans Don't," *Bloomberg*, June 24, 215, https://www.bloomberg.com/news/articles/2015-06-24/do-you-know-what-your-spouse-makes-43-percent-of-americans-don-t.

7. Burn Your Mortgage

19 Andrea Hopkins, "Indebted Canadians Using 'Homes as ATMs,' Consumer Agency Warns," *Global News*, June 7, 2017, https://globalnews.ca/news/3510435/canadians-homes-as-atms/.

20 Garry Marr, "Half of Canadians Plan to Retire with Mortgage: Survey," *Financial Post*, May 16, 2012, https://business.financialpost.com/personal-finance/mortgages-real-estate/half-of-canadians-plan-to-retire-with-mortgage-survey.

21 "Mortgage Payment Calculator Canada," Ratehub.ca, accessed July 29, 2019, https://www.ratehub.ca/mortgage-payment-calculator.

22 "Mortgage Pre-Payment Calculator," Firstfoundation.ca, accessed July 29, 2019, https://www.firstfoundation.ca/mortgage/calculators/prepayment/.

8. Going Solo

23 Erica Alini, "The Cost of Raising a Child? Now There's a Calculator for That," *Global News*, June 14, 2018, https://globalnews.ca/news/4271482/canada-child-cost-calculator/.

24 "Payday Loans: Market Trends," Government of Canada, April 28, 2017, https://www.canada.ca/en/financial-consumer-agency/programs/research/payday-loans-market-trends.html

25 "FCAC Report: Consumers' Knowledge and Use of Home Equity Lines of Credit Puts Their Financial Well-Being at Risk," *News Wire*, January 15, 2019, https://www.newswire.ca/news-releases/fcac-report-consumers-knowledge-and-use-of-home-equity-lines-of-credit-puts-their-financial-well-being-at-risk-880956358.html.

26 "Child-care Costs in Canada Among Highest in the World, OECD Says," CBC.ca, October 21, 2016, https://www.cbc.ca/news/business/oecd-child-care-costs-1.3815954.

27 Leslie Young, "More Canadians Using Payday Loans, Most Don't Understand Costs: Report," *Global News*, October 25, 2016, https:// globalnews.ca/news/3025310/more-canadians-using-payday -loans-most-dont-understand-costs-report/.

28 Ibid.

29 GreedyRates, "Compare Personal Loan Rates in Canada," Greedy Rates.ca, May 30, 2019, https://www.greedyrates.ca/blog/com paring-personal-loans-canada/.

30 "Line 214—Child Care Expenses," Government of Canada, February 12, 2019, https://www.canada.ca/en/revenue-agency/services /tax/individuals/topics/about-your-tax-return/tax-return /completing-a-tax-return/deductions-credits-expenses/line -214-child-care-expenses.html.

31 "The Canada Child Benefit," Government of Canada, May 16, 2019, https://www.canada.ca/en/employment-social-development /campaigns/canada-child-benefit.html.

32 "National Child Benefit," Government of Canada, October 18, 2016, https://www.canada.ca/en/employment-social-development /programs/child-benefit.html.

33 "Child Disability Benefit," Government of Canada, November 16, 2018, https://www.canada.ca/en/revenue-agency/services/child -family-benefits/child-disability-benefit.html.

34 Pete Evans, "Food Waste Costs Canada $31B a Year, Report Says," CBC.ca, December 11, 2014, https://www.cbc.ca/news /business/food-waste-costs-canada-31b-a-year-report-says -1.2869708.

35 "Study shows many Canadians vulnerable to a personal financial crisis," Edward Jones, March 2, 2017, https://www .edwardjones.ca/about/media/news-releases/study-shows -many-canadians-vulnerable-to-a-personal-financial-crisis .html.

36 "The Ontario Tax Brackets and Personal Marginal Income Tax Rates," *Easy Tax Canada*, accessed July 29, 2019, https://easy taxca.com/tax-brackets-and-marginal-tax-rates-in-canada/on tario-personal-marginal-income-tax-rates-2/.

9. The Sandwich Generation

37 James Langton, "Canadians Missing Out on Tax Breaks for Caregivers: Poll," *Investigative Executive*, August 22, 2018, https://www.investmentexecutive.com/news/industry-news/canadians-missing-out-on-tax-breaks-for-caregivers-poll/.

10. The Pandemic and Business Ownership

38 Sean Simpson, "Eight in Ten (77%) Canadians Have Wanted to Be Their Own Boss," Ipsos, October 10, 2016, https://www.ipsos.com/en-ca/news-polls/eight-ten-77-canadians-have-wanted-be-their-own-boss; Margie McNeil and Angela Gordon, "Being the 'Boss of Me' Appeals to Canadians: RBCPoll," RBC, May 25, 2011, http://www.rbc.com/newsroom/news/2011/20110525-entrepreneurs.html.

39 Sara Mojtehedzadeh, "While Banks Slash Their Rates on Loans, Many Payday Lenders Are Still Charging as Much as They Can," *Toronto Star*, April 11, 2020, https://www.thestar.com/business/2020/04/11/amidst-a-pandemic-some-payday-lenders-are-limiting-services-others-are-expanding-them.html.

40 See note 38.

41 Steve Randall, "How Much Does the Average Canadian Save?" *Wealth Professional*, March 28, 2019, https://www.wealthprofessional.ca/news/industry-news/how-much-does-the-average-canadian-save/255921.

42 Mike Vlasveld, "ACORN Ottawa Calling for Extension of Ontario Rent Forgiveness and Eviction Moratorium," OttawaMatters.com, July 22, 2020, https://www.ottawamatters.com/local-news/acorn-ottawa-calling-for-extension-of-ontario-rent-forgiveness-and-eviction-memorandum-2582884.

43 "Payday Loans," Government of Canada, May 15, 2020, https://www.canada.ca/en/financial-consumer-agency/services/loans/payday-loans.html.

44 Ibid.

11. COVID and Your Family Finances

45 Anita Balakrishnan, "Why Anyone Who Deferred Mortgage Payments Should Check Their Credit Score," *Canadian Investor*, August 13, 2020, https://www.canadianinvestor.com/2020/08/13 /why-anyone-who-deferred-mortgage-payments-should-check -their-credit-score; Tim Bennett, "New CMHC Rules May Make Mortgage Applications Tougher," Ratehub.ca, June 4, 2020, https://www.ratehub.ca/blog/new-cmhc-rules-covid-19.

About the Author

© SANDRA MONACO

Kelley Keehn's second language is money and her mission is to make Canadians feel good about it. A veteran in the industry, she's spent fifteen years as a personal financial educator and over a decade as a financial professional, and she's learned that everyone has money problems. That's as true for millionaires as it is for people who spend years trying to pay off their student debt.

As an award-winning, bestselling author of ten books that cover topics including personal finance, the psychology of money, behavioural economics, women and finance, and avoiding identity fraud, she knows what's on the minds and in the hearts of Canadians when it comes to their bank accounts.

As a speaker, consultant, and media personality, Kelley used to regularly travel across the country, empowering the financial industry, major corporations, and consumers to make more informed financial decisions. Now, because of the pandemic, she connects with companies, individuals, and media around the globe from her home studio and dreams of seeing Canadians in person again, one day soon.

Kelley is the financial authority for *The Marilyn Denis Show*, as well as a regular guest on Global, CBC, and CTV. She was the host of the W Network's *Burn My Mortgage*, a CNBC New York contributor, and a *Globe and Mail* columnist, and she has made thousands of international radio and TV appearances over the course of her career.

Kelley is proud to have served as the Consumer Advocate for FP Canada and was a member of the first National Steering Committee on Financial Literacy. Today, she serves on the Ontario Securities Commission Seniors Expert Advisory Committee, the Canadian Foundation for Economic Education, and the Financial Consumer Agency of Canada's Consumer Protection Advisory Committee and is an affiliate member of the OECD's International Network on Financial Education.

Visit her online at **KelleyKeehn.com** and **@KelleyKeehn**.